Crystals and Spells

A Practical Spellbook of Crystal Magic

by
Witchcraft Magick

<u>*Introduction*</u>

Crystals have fascinated humanity for centuries, celebrated not only for their mesmerizing beauty but also for their profound metaphysical properties. These natural wonders are believed to embody unique energies that can amplify our intentions, shield us from negativity, and facilitate spiritual and emotional healing. This spell book serves as a guide into the enchanting realm of crystals, offering a comprehensive compendium of spells and rituals to enrich and elevate your spiritual practice.

Within these pages, you will embark on a journey through the diverse and mystical world of crystals. Each section is dedicated to a specific crystal, providing an insightful exploration into its historical significance, elemental composition, and metaphysical attributes. While offering an overview rather than an in-depth analysis, these introductions aim to illuminate the essence of each crystal and its relevance in spiritual and holistic practices.

Whether you seek protection, love, prosperity, or personal transformation, the spells contained herein are crafted to harness the inherent energies of each crystal. From ancient civilizations to modern mystics, crystals have been revered for their ability to align energies, awaken inner wisdom, and enhance one's connection with the natural world. By integrating these spells into your daily rituals, you can unlock the potent potential of crystals to manifest your desires and illuminate your spiritual path.

Amethyst

Rose Quartz

Clear Quartz

Black Tourmaline

Citrine

Tiger's Eye

Selenite

Hematite

Lapis Lazuli

Carnelian

Aventurine

Labradorite

Smoky Quartz

Garnet

Aquamarine

Moonstone

Ruby

Obsidian

Emerald

Peridot

Amazonite

Opal

Jade

Amethyst

Introduction to Amethyst

Amethyst is a powerful crystal known for its protective, healing, and purifying properties. Used by ancient civilizations for its spiritual and healing properties, amethyst continues to be a favorite among crystal enthusiasts. It typically appears in shades of purple, ranging from light lavender to deep violet.

Properties and Uses of Amethyst

Amethyst is renowned for its healing properties. It calms the mind, reduces stress, and promotes emotional balance. As a protective crystal, amethyst shields against negative energies and psychic attacks. Spiritually, it enhances awareness and intuition. Common uses include meditation, protection, and healing rituals.

Cleansing and Charging Amethyst

Cleansing your amethyst is essential to maintain its effectiveness. You can cleanse it using water, by placing it under moonlight, or by smudging with sage. Charging amethyst can be done by exposing it to sunlight, moonlight, or through intention setting.

Amethyst Spells

Calming Spell

Purpose: To reduce stress and anxiety.

Materials: Amethyst, lavender candle.

Instructions: Light the lavender candle, hold the amethyst, and visualize calm energy surrounding you.

Protection Spell

Purpose: To protect against negative energies.

Materials: Amethyst, black candle.

Instructions: Light the black candle, place the amethyst near it, and visualize a protective shield forming around you.

Healing Spell

Purpose: To promote physical and emotional healing.

Materials: Amethyst, white candle, healing herbs.

Instructions: Light the white candle, hold the amethyst, and visualize healing energy flowing through you.

Intuition Enhancement Spell

Purpose: To enhance intuition and psychic abilities.

Materials: Amethyst, indigo candle.

Instructions: Light the indigo candle, meditate with the amethyst, and focus on enhancing your intuitive abilities.

Sleep Spell

Purpose: To promote restful sleep.

Materials: Amethyst, chamomile tea, blue candle.

Instructions: Light the blue candle, place the amethyst under your pillow, and drink chamomile tea before bed.

Emotional Balance Spell

Purpose: To achieve emotional stability.

Materials: Amethyst, pink candle.

Instructions: Light the pink candle, hold the amethyst, and visualize balanced and stable emotions.

Dream Clarity Spell

Purpose: To enhance the clarity of dreams.

Materials: Amethyst, dream journal, purple candle.

Instructions: Light the purple candle, place the amethyst near your bed, and keep a dream journal.

Energy Cleansing Spell

Purpose: To cleanse your personal energy.

Materials: Amethyst, sage bundle, white candle.

Instructions: Light the white candle, burn the sage, and pass the amethyst through the smoke while visualizing cleansing.

Meditation Enhancement Spell

Purpose: To deepen meditation practices.

Materials: Amethyst, meditation cushion, incense.

Instructions: Sit on your meditation cushion, hold the amethyst, and burn incense while meditating.

Focus and Clarity Spell

Purpose: To improve focus and mental clarity.

Materials: Amethyst, yellow candle.

Instructions: Light the yellow candle, hold the amethyst, and focus on clear and focused thoughts.

Spiritual Awakening Spell

Purpose: To promote spiritual awakening.

Materials: Amethyst, white candle, sacred herbs.

Instructions: Light the white candle, hold the amethyst, and burn sacred herbs while focusing on spiritual awakening.

Aura Protection Spell

Purpose: To protect your aura.

Materials: Amethyst, black tourmaline, purple candle.

Instructions: Light the purple candle, place the amethyst and black tourmaline near you, and visualize a protective aura.

Creativity Boost Spell

Purpose: To enhance creativity.

Materials: Amethyst, orange candle, art supplies.

Instructions: Light the orange candle, hold the amethyst, and engage in creative activities.

Love and Compassion Spell

Purpose: To foster love and compassion.

Materials: Amethyst, rose quartz, pink candle.

Instructions: Light the pink candle, hold the amethyst and rose quartz, and visualize love and compassion.

Manifestation Spell

Purpose: To manifest your desires.

Materials: Amethyst, green candle, manifestation journal.

Instructions: Light the green candle, hold the amethyst, and write your desires in the journal.

Spiritual Connection Spell

Purpose: To connect with higher realms.

Materials: Amethyst, blue candle, sacred symbols.

Instructions: Light the blue candle, hold the amethyst, and meditate on connecting with higher realms.

Self-Discovery Spell

Purpose: To promote self-discovery.

Materials: Amethyst, yellow candle, journal.

Instructions: Light the yellow candle, hold the amethyst, and journal about self-discovery.

Energy Protection Spell

Purpose: To protect your energy field.

Materials: Amethyst, black candle, protective herbs.

Instructions: Light the black candle, hold the amethyst, and burn protective herbs while focusing on energy protection.

Peace and Tranquility Spell

Purpose: To create a peaceful environment.

Materials: Amethyst, blue candle, calming music.

Instructions: Light the blue candle, hold the amethyst, and play calming music.

Grounding Spell

Purpose: To ground yourself.

Materials: Amethyst, brown candle, earth element (soil, rock).

Instructions: Light the brown candle, hold the amethyst, and focus on grounding yourself with the earth element.

Self-Love Spell

Purpose: To enhance self-love.

Materials: Amethyst, rose quartz, pink candle.

Instructions: Light the pink candle, hold the amethyst and rose quartz, and focus on self-love.

Anxiety Relief Spell

Purpose: To relieve anxiety.

Materials: Amethyst, lavender candle, calming tea.

Instructions: Light the lavender candle, hold the amethyst, and drink calming tea while visualizing anxiety relief.

Focus and Concentration Spell

Purpose: To improve concentration.

Materials: Amethyst, yellow candle, study materials.

Instructions: Light the yellow candle, hold the amethyst, and focus on your study materials.

Positive Energy Spell

Purpose: To attract positive energy.

Materials: Amethyst, white candle, positive affirmations.

Instructions: Light the white candle, hold the amethyst, and recite positive affirmations.

Transformation Spell

Purpose: To promote personal transformation.

Materials: Amethyst, purple candle, transformation journal.

Instructions: Light the purple candle, hold the amethyst, and write about your desired transformation in the journal.

Amethyst is a versatile and powerful crystal with a wide range of applications. By incorporating these spells into your practice, you can tap into its energy for protection, healing, and spiritual growth. Remember to personalize these spells and explore your unique connection with amethyst.

Rose Quartz

Introduction to Rose Quartz

Rose quartz is known as the stone of unconditional love. This beautiful pink crystal has been cherished throughout history for its powerful energy that promotes love, compassion, and emotional healing. Rose quartz is often associated with the heart chakra, making it a popular choice for enhancing relationships and self-love.

Properties and Uses of Rose Quartz

Rose quartz is renowned for its ability to attract love, heal emotional wounds, and promote inner peace. It is a nurturing crystal that encourages compassion and forgiveness. Common uses include enhancing romantic relationships, fostering self-love, and soothing emotional turmoil.

Cleansing and Charging Rose Quartz

Cleansing rose quartz can be done using water, by placing it under moonlight, or by smudging with sage. Charging this crystal can be achieved by exposing it to sunlight, moonlight, or through intention setting.

Rose Quartz Spells

Joy and Happiness Spell

Purpose: To attract joy and happiness.

Materials: Rose quartz, yellow candle, sunflowers.

Instructions: Light the yellow candle, place the rose quartz and sunflowers around it. Visualize the energy of the rose quartz bringing joy and happiness into your life.

Forgiveness Spell

Purpose: To promote forgiveness.

Materials: Rose quartz, white candle.

Instructions: Light the white candle, hold the rose quartz, and focus on the person or situation you need to forgive. Visualize the energy of forgiveness flowing from the rose quartz into your heart.

Healing Relationships Spell

Purpose: To heal and improve relationships.

Materials: Rose quartz, pink candle, photo of the person.

Instructions: Light the pink candle, hold the rose quartz, and focus on the photo of the person you wish to heal your relationship with. Visualize the energy of the rose quartz healing and improving your relationship.

Relationship Harmony Spell

Purpose: To enhance harmony in relationships.

Materials: Rose quartz, green candle, picture of you and your partner.

Instructions: Light the green candle, place the picture and rose quartz in front of it. Visualize harmony and love flowing between you and your partner.

Self-Love Spell

Purpose: To enhance self-love.

Materials: Rose quartz, pink candle, mirror.

Instructions: Light the pink candle, hold the rose quartz, and look into the mirror. Speak words of love and affirmation to yourself, visualizing the energy of the rose quartz enhancing your self-love.

Emotional Strength Spell

Purpose: To enhance emotional strength.

Materials: Rose quartz, red candle.

Instructions: Light the red candle, hold the rose quartz, and visualize the energy of the crystal enhancing your emotional strength.

Emotional Healing Spell

Purpose: To heal emotional wounds.

Materials: Rose quartz, lavender candle, journal.

Instructions: Light the lavender candle, hold the rose quartz, and write in your journal about your emotions. Visualize the rose quartz healing your emotional wounds as you express your feelings.

Compassion Spell

Purpose: To increase compassion.

Materials: Rose quartz, blue candle.

Instructions: Light the blue candle, hold the rose quartz, and visualize the energy of compassion flowing from the crystal into your heart.

Love Attraction Spell

Purpose: To attract love.

Materials: Rose quartz, pink candle, rose petals.

Instructions: Light the pink candle and place the rose quartz in front of it. Surround the crystal with rose petals. As you do this, focus on the feeling of love and visualize it entering your life.

Attract Friendship Spell

Purpose: To attract new friendships.

Materials: Rose quartz, yellow candle, pink flowers.

Instructions: Light the yellow candle, place the rose quartz and pink flowers around it. Visualize new, positive friendships coming into your life.

Heart Chakra Balancing Spell

Purpose: To balance the heart chakra.

Materials: Rose quartz, green candle.

Instructions: Light the green candle, hold the rose quartz over your heart chakra, and visualize a green light balancing and healing your heart chakra.

Stress Relief Spell

Purpose: To relieve stress.

Materials: Rose quartz, white candle, lavender essential oil.

Instructions: Light the white candle, apply a few drops of lavender essential oil to the rose quartz, and hold the crystal while taking deep breaths, visualizing stress leaving your body.

Dream Enhancement Spell

Purpose: To enhance the quality of dreams.

Materials: Rose quartz, dream journal, purple candle.

Instructions: Light the purple candle, place the rose quartz under your pillow, and keep a dream journal by your bed. Visualize the energy of the rose quartz enhancing your dreams.

Romantic Love Spell

Purpose: To enhance romantic love.

Materials: Rose quartz, red candle, chocolate.

Instructions: Light the red candle, hold the rose quartz, and share a piece of chocolate with your partner. Visualize the energy of the rose quartz deepening your romantic love.

Inner Peace Spell

Purpose: To promote inner peace.

Materials: Rose quartz, white candle, calming music.

Instructions: Light the white candle, hold the rose quartz, and play calming music. Visualize the energy of the rose quartz bringing you inner peace.

Gratitude Spell

Purpose: To foster gratitude.

Materials: Rose quartz, white candle, gratitude journal.

Instructions: Light the white candle, hold the rose quartz, and write in your gratitude journal. Visualize the energy of the rose quartz enhancing your feelings of gratitude.

Peaceful Home Spell

Purpose: To create a peaceful home environment.

Materials: Rose quartz, white candle, sage.

Instructions: Light the white candle, hold the rose quartz, and smudge your home with sage while visualizing a peaceful environment.

Protection from Emotional Harm Spell

Purpose: To protect from emotional harm.

Materials: Rose quartz, black candle.

Instructions: Light the black candle, hold the rose quartz, and visualize a protective shield forming around you, guarding against emotional harm.

Gentle Energy Spell

Purpose: To bring gentle and nurturing energy.

Materials: Rose quartz, blue candle.

Instructions: Light the blue candle, hold the rose quartz, and visualize the gentle energy of the crystal surrounding you.

Inspiration Spell

Purpose: To inspire creativity and new ideas.

Materials: Rose quartz, orange candle, creative tools (pen, paper, art supplies).

Instructions: Light the orange candle, hold the rose quartz, and engage in a creative activity, visualizing the energy of the crystal inspiring new ideas.

Healing from Heartbreak Spell

Purpose: To heal from heartbreak.

Materials: Rose quartz, pink candle, journal.

Instructions: Light the pink candle, hold the rose quartz, and write about your feelings in your journal. Visualize the energy of the rose quartz healing your heart.

Acceptance Spell

Purpose: To promote acceptance.

Materials: Rose quartz, white candle.

Instructions: Light the white candle, hold the rose quartz, and focus on accepting yourself and others, visualizing the energy of the crystal fostering acceptance.

Beauty Spell

Purpose: To enhance inner and outer beauty.

Materials: Rose quartz, pink candle, beauty products.

Instructions: Light the pink candle, hold the rose quartz, and use your beauty products while visualizing the energy of the crystal enhancing your beauty.

Peaceful Sleep Spell

Purpose: To promote peaceful sleep.

Materials: Rose quartz, lavender candle, lavender sachet.

Instructions: Light the lavender candle, place the rose quartz and lavender sachet under your pillow, and visualize peaceful sleep.

Confidence Spell

Purpose: To boost confidence.

Materials: Rose quartz, yellow candle, mirror.

Instructions: Light the yellow candle, hold the rose quartz, and look into the mirror, speaking words of confidence and affirmation to yourself.

Rose quartz is a nurturing and powerful crystal with a wide range of applications. By incorporating these spells into your practice, you can tap into its energy for love, healing, and emotional balance. Remember to personalize these spells and explore your unique connection with rose quartz.

Clear Quartz

Introduction to Clear Quartz

Clear quartz, often referred to as the "master healer," is a versatile and powerful crystal known for its ability to amplify energy and intentions. This crystal is colorless and transparent, often appearing like ice or glass. Clear quartz is highly regarded in the world of crystal healing for its adaptability and effectiveness.

Properties and Uses of Clear Quartz

Clear quartz has the unique ability to enhance the energies of other crystals and amplify intentions. It is known for its healing properties, clarity of thought, and energy purification. Common uses include meditation, energy amplification, and healing rituals.

Cleansing and Charging Clear Quartz

Cleansing clear quartz can be done using water, by placing it under moonlight, or by smudging with sage. Charging this crystal can be achieved by exposing it to sunlight, moonlight, or through intention setting.

Clear Quartz Spells

Energy Amplification Spell

Purpose: To amplify personal energy and intentions.

Materials: Clear quartz, white candle.

Instructions: Light the white candle, hold the clear quartz, and focus on your intentions, visualizing them being amplified by the energy of the crystal.

Clarity of Mind Spell

Purpose: To achieve mental clarity.

Materials: Clear quartz, yellow candle, rosemary.

Instructions: Light the yellow candle, place the clear quartz and rosemary in front of it. Visualize the energy of the clear quartz bringing clarity to your thoughts.

Healing Spell

Purpose: To promote physical and emotional healing.

Materials: Clear quartz, green candle, healing herbs.

Instructions: Light the green candle, hold the clear quartz, and visualize healing energy flowing through you.

Meditation Enhancement Spell

Purpose: To deepen meditation practices.

Materials: Clear quartz, blue candle, incense.

Instructions: Light the blue candle, hold the clear quartz, and burn incense while meditating.

Manifestation Spell

Purpose: To manifest desires.

Materials: Clear quartz, purple candle, manifestation journal.

Instructions: Light the purple candle, hold the clear quartz, and write your desires in the journal, visualizing them coming to fruition.

Protection Spell

Purpose: To protect against negative energies.

Materials: Clear quartz, black candle.

Instructions: Light the black candle, place the clear quartz near it, and visualize a protective shield forming around you.

Spiritual Growth Spell

Purpose: To promote spiritual growth.

Materials: Clear quartz, white candle, sacred symbols.

Instructions: Light the white candle, hold the clear quartz, and meditate on connecting with higher realms and spiritual growth.

Focus and Concentration Spell

Purpose: To improve focus and mental clarity.

Materials: Clear quartz, yellow candle.

Instructions: Light the yellow candle, hold the clear quartz, and focus on clear and focused thoughts.

Aura Cleansing Spell

Purpose: To cleanse and purify the aura.

Materials: Clear quartz, white candle, sage bundle.

Instructions: Light the white candle, burn the sage, and pass the clear quartz through the smoke while visualizing cleansing.

Energy Balancing Spell

Purpose: To balance personal energy.

Materials: Clear quartz, blue candle.

Instructions: Light the blue candle, hold the clear quartz, and visualize balancing your personal energy.

Creativity Boost Spell

Purpose: To enhance creativity.

Materials: Clear quartz, orange candle, art supplies.

Instructions: Light the orange candle, hold the clear quartz, and engage in creative activities, visualizing inspiration flowing through you.

Inner Peace Spell

Purpose: To promote inner peace.

Materials: Clear quartz, white candle, calming music.

Instructions: Light the white candle, hold the clear quartz, and play calming music. Visualize the energy of the clear quartz bringing you inner peace.

Positive Energy Spell

Purpose: To attract positive energy.

Materials: Clear quartz, white candle, positive affirmations.

Instructions: Light the white candle, hold the clear quartz, and recite positive affirmations.

Spiritual Connection Spell

Purpose: To connect with higher realms.

Materials: Clear quartz, blue candle, sacred symbols.

Instructions: Light the blue candle, hold the clear quartz, and meditate on connecting with higher realms.

Self-Discovery Spell

Purpose: To promote self-discovery.

Materials: Clear quartz, yellow candle, journal.

Instructions: Light the yellow candle, hold the clear quartz, and journal about self-discovery.

Energy Protection Spell

Purpose: To protect your energy field.

Materials: Clear quartz, black candle, protective herbs.

Instructions: Light the black candle, hold the clear quartz, and burn protective herbs while focusing on energy protection.

Peace and Tranquility Spell

Purpose: To create a peaceful environment.

Materials: Clear quartz, blue candle, calming music.

Instructions: Light the blue candle, hold the clear quartz, and play calming music.

Grounding Spell

Purpose: To ground yourself.

Materials: Clear quartz, brown candle, earth element (soil, rock).

Instructions: Light the brown candle, hold the clear quartz, and focus on grounding yourself with the earth element.

Confidence Spell

Purpose: To boost confidence.

Materials: Clear quartz, yellow candle, mirror.

Instructions: Light the yellow candle, hold the clear quartz, and look into the mirror, speaking words of confidence and affirmation to yourself.

Transformation Spell

Purpose: To promote personal transformation.

Materials: Clear quartz, purple candle, transformation journal.

Instructions: Light the purple candle, hold the clear quartz, and write about your desired transformation in the journal.

Calming Spell

Purpose: To reduce stress and anxiety.

Materials: Clear quartz, lavender candle.

Instructions: Light the lavender candle, hold the clear quartz, and visualize calm energy surrounding you.

Dream Clarity Spell

Purpose: To enhance the clarity of dreams.

Materials: Clear quartz, dream journal, purple candle.

Instructions: Light the purple candle, place the clear quartz near your bed, and keep a dream journal.

Energy Cleansing Spell

Purpose: To cleanse your personal energy.

Materials: Clear quartz, sage bundle, white candle.

Instructions: Light the white candle, burn the sage, and pass the clear quartz through the smoke while visualizing cleansing.

Healing Relationships Spell

Purpose: To heal and improve relationships.

Materials: Clear quartz, pink candle, photo of the person.

Instructions: Light the pink candle, hold the clear quartz, and focus on the photo of the person you wish to heal your relationship with. Visualize the energy of the clear quartz healing and improving your relationship.

Joy and Happiness Spell

Purpose: To attract joy and happiness.

Materials: Clear quartz, yellow candle, sunflowers.

Instructions: Light the yellow candle, place the clear quartz and sunflowers around it. Visualize the energy of the clear quartz bringing joy and happiness into your life.

Clear quartz is an exceptionally versatile crystal, capable of amplifying energies and intentions. Through these spells, you can harness its power for healing, clarity, and spiritual growth. Explore your unique connection with clear quartz and personalize these spells to suit your needs. Each experience with clear quartz will deepen your understanding and enhance your magical practice.

Black Tourmaline

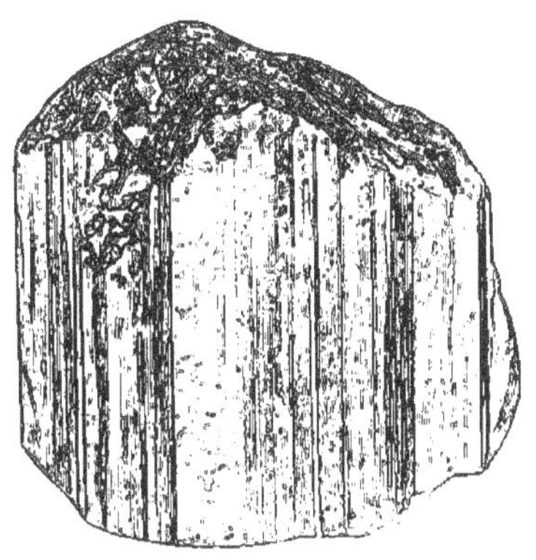

Introduction to Black Tourmaline

Black tourmaline is a powerful protective stone known for its ability to shield against negative energies and electromagnetic radiation. This deep black crystal is highly regarded for its grounding and purifying properties. It has been used for centuries as a talisman of protection and a grounding force.

Properties and Uses of Black Tourmaline

Black tourmaline is renowned for its ability to protect against negativity and psychic attacks. It is a grounding stone that connects you to the Earth, promoting a sense of stability and security. Common uses include protection, grounding, and energy purification rituals.

Cleansing and Charging Black Tourmaline

Cleansing black tourmaline can be done using water, by placing it under moonlight, or by smudging with sage. Charging this crystal can be achieved by exposing it to sunlight, moonlight, or through intention setting.

Black Tourmaline Spells

Protection Spell

Purpose: To protect against negative energies.

Materials: Black tourmaline, black candle.

Instructions: Light the black candle, hold the black tourmaline, and visualize a protective shield forming around you.

Grounding Spell

Purpose: To ground yourself.

Materials: Black tourmaline, brown candle, earth element (soil, rock).

Instructions: Light the brown candle, hold the black tourmaline, and focus on grounding yourself with the earth element.

Energy Cleansing Spell

Purpose: To cleanse your personal energy.

Materials: Black tourmaline, sage bundle, white candle.

Instructions: Light the white candle, burn the sage, and pass the black tourmaline through the smoke while visualizing cleansing.

Electromagnetic Protection Spell

Purpose: To protect against electromagnetic radiation.

Materials: Black tourmaline, blue candle, electronic devices.

Instructions: Light the blue candle, place the black tourmaline near your electronic devices, and visualize it absorbing and deflecting harmful radiation.

Anxiety Relief Spell

Purpose: To relieve anxiety.

Materials: Black tourmaline, lavender candle, calming tea.

Instructions: Light the lavender candle, hold the black tourmaline, and drink calming tea while visualizing anxiety leaving your body.

Emotional Stability Spell

Purpose: To achieve emotional stability.

Materials: Black tourmaline, pink candle.

Instructions: Light the pink candle, hold the black tourmaline, and visualize balanced and stable emotions.

Spiritual Protection Spell

Purpose: To protect against psychic attacks.

Materials: Black tourmaline, purple candle.

Instructions: Light the purple candle, hold the black tourmaline, and visualize a protective barrier forming around your spirit.

Home Protection Spell

Purpose: To protect your home.

Materials: Black tourmaline, white candle, salt.

Instructions: Light the white candle, place black tourmaline near entrances, and sprinkle salt around doorways and windows while visualizing protection.

Stress Reduction Spell

Purpose: To reduce stress.

Materials: Black tourmaline, blue candle, calming music.

Instructions: Light the blue candle, hold the black tourmaline, and play calming music while visualizing stress leaving your body.

Focus and Concentration Spell

Purpose: To improve focus and mental clarity.

Materials: Black tourmaline, yellow candle.

Instructions: Light the yellow candle, hold the black tourmaline, and focus on clear and focused thoughts.

Sleep Protection Spell

Purpose: To protect against nightmares.

Materials: Black tourmaline, blue candle, lavender sachet.

Instructions: Light the blue candle, place the black tourmaline and lavender sachet under your pillow, and visualize peaceful sleep.

Energy Shield Spell

Purpose: To create an energy shield.

Materials: Black tourmaline, white candle.

Instructions: Light the white candle, hold the black tourmaline, and visualize an energy shield surrounding you.

Physical Healing Spell

Purpose: To promote physical healing.

Materials: Black tourmaline, green candle, healing herbs.

Instructions: Light the green candle, hold the black tourmaline, and visualize healing energy flowing through you.

Aura Protection Spell

Purpose: To protect your aura.

Materials: Black tourmaline, purple candle, sage.

Instructions: Light the purple candle, burn sage, and pass the black tourmaline through the smoke while visualizing aura protection.

Self-Confidence Spell

Purpose: To boost self-confidence.

Materials: Black tourmaline, yellow candle, mirror.

Instructions: Light the yellow candle, hold the black tourmaline, and look into the mirror, speaking words of confidence and affirmation to yourself.

Inner Strength Spell

Purpose: To enhance inner strength.

Materials: Black tourmaline, red candle.

Instructions: Light the red candle, hold the black tourmaline, and visualize the energy of the crystal enhancing your inner strength.

Energy Clearing Spell

Purpose: To clear negative energy.

Materials: Black tourmaline, white candle, bell or chime.

Instructions: Light the white candle, hold the black tourmaline, and ring the bell or chime while visualizing negative energy being cleared away.

Travel Protection Spell

Purpose: To protect while traveling.

Materials: Black tourmaline, white candle, travel token.

Instructions: Light the white candle, hold the black tourmaline, and place the travel token next to it, visualizing safe travels.

Grounding Meditation Spell

Purpose: To enhance grounding during meditation.

Materials: Black tourmaline, meditation cushion, incense.

Instructions: Sit on your meditation cushion, hold the black tourmaline, and burn incense while meditating on grounding energy.

Protection from Negative Influences Spell

Purpose: To protect against negative influences.

Materials: Black tourmaline, black candle.

Instructions: Light the black candle, hold the black tourmaline, and visualize a barrier protecting you from negative influences.

Calm and Tranquility Spell

Purpose: To promote calm and tranquility.

Materials: Black tourmaline, blue candle, chamomile tea.

Instructions: Light the blue candle, hold the black tourmaline, and drink chamomile tea while visualizing calm and tranquility.

Empowerment Spell

Purpose: To feel empowered.

Materials: Black tourmaline, yellow candle.

Instructions: Light the yellow candle, hold the black tourmaline, and visualize the energy of the crystal empowering you.

Peaceful Home Environment Spell

Purpose: To create a peaceful home environment.

Materials: Black tourmaline, white candle, sage.

Instructions: Light the white candle, hold the black tourmaline, and smudge your home with sage while visualizing a peaceful environment.

Self-Discovery Spell

Purpose: To promote self-discovery.

Materials: Black tourmaline, yellow candle, journal.

Instructions: Light the yellow candle, hold the black tourmaline, and journal about self-discovery.

Positive Energy Spell

Purpose: To attract positive energy.

Materials: Black tourmaline, white candle, positive affirmations.

Instructions: Light the white candle, hold the black tourmaline, and recite positive affirmations.

Black tourmaline is a grounding and protective crystal with profound capabilities. By integrating these spells into your practice, you can harness its energy for protection, grounding, and purification. Embrace the strength of black tourmaline, and let it guide you in building a safe and balanced life. With each spell, deepen your connection to this powerful stone and allow its grounding energy to support you on your journey.

Citrine

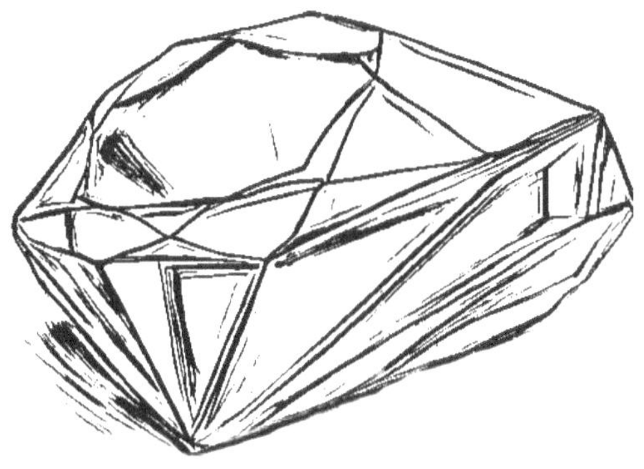

Introduction to Citrine

Citrine is a radiant yellow crystal known for its joyful energy and powerful manifestation properties. Often called the "merchant's stone," Citrine is associated with abundance, prosperity, and success. Its sunny disposition uplifts the spirit and encourages positivity in all aspects of life.

Properties and Uses of Citrine

Citrine is renowned for its ability to attract wealth, prosperity, and success. It is a stone of manifestation, helping you bring your dreams and desires into reality. Common uses include attracting abundance, enhancing creativity, and promoting optimism and self-confidence.

Cleansing and Charging Citrine

Citrine can be cleansed by placing it under running water, burying it in a bowl of dry sea salt, or smudging it with sage. Charging this crystal can be done by placing it in sunlight or moonlight, or by visualizing bright, golden light infusing it with positive energy.

<u>Citrine Spells</u>

Abundance Attraction Spell

Purpose: To attract abundance and prosperity.

Materials: Citrine, green candle.

Instructions: Light the green candle, hold the Citrine, and visualize streams of abundance flowing into your life.

Success in Business Spell

Purpose: To enhance success in business ventures.

Materials: Citrine, gold candle, business plan.

Instructions: Light the gold candle, hold the Citrine, and visualize your business thriving and growing.

Manifestation Spell

Purpose: To manifest desires into reality.

Materials: Citrine, purple candle, manifestation journal.

Instructions: Light the purple candle, hold the Citrine, and write down your desires in the manifestation journal while visualizing them coming true.

Energy Cleansing Spell

Purpose: To cleanse your personal energy.

Materials: Citrine, sage bundle, white candle.

Instructions: Light the white candle, burn the sage, and pass the Citrine through the smoke while visualizing cleansing and purification.

Confidence Boost Spell

Purpose: To boost self-confidence and positivity.

Materials: Citrine, yellow candle.

Instructions: Light the yellow candle, hold the Citrine, and affirm your self-worth and confidence.

Creativity Flow Spell

Purpose: To enhance creativity and inspiration.

Materials: Citrine, orange candle, artistic tools.

Instructions: Light the orange candle, hold the Citrine, and engage in creative activities while feeling inspired.

Joy and Happiness Spell

Purpose: To attract joy and happiness.

Materials: Citrine, pink candle.

Instructions: Light the pink candle, hold the Citrine, and visualize joy and happiness filling your life.

Prosperity Spell

Purpose: To attract overall prosperity.

Materials: Citrine, green candle, prosperity herbs (such as basil or cinnamon).

Instructions: Light the green candle, hold the Citrine, and sprinkle prosperity herbs around it while visualizing a life of prosperity.

Optimism Spell

Purpose: To foster optimism and positive thinking.

Materials: Citrine, yellow candle.

Instructions: Light the yellow candle, hold the Citrine, and surround yourself with thoughts of optimism and positivity.

Wealth Accumulation Spell

Purpose: To attract wealth and financial stability.

Materials: Citrine, gold candle, coins or money symbol.

Instructions: Light the gold candle, hold the Citrine, and place coins or money symbols near it while visualizing wealth flowing into your life.

Protection from Negative Energies Spell

Purpose: To protect against negative energies.

Materials: Citrine, black candle.

Instructions: Light the black candle, hold the Citrine, and visualize a shield of protective light surrounding you.

Decision Making Spell

Purpose: To aid in making clear decisions.

Materials: Citrine, blue candle, list of options.

Instructions: Light the blue candle, hold the Citrine, and focus on gaining clarity and insight into your decisions.

Health and Vitality Spell

Purpose: To promote health and vitality.

Materials: Citrine, green candle, healing herbs.

Instructions: Light the green candle, hold the Citrine, and visualize healing energy flowing through your body.

Harmony in Relationships Spell

Purpose: To promote harmony and understanding in relationships.

Materials: Citrine, pink candle, photo of loved ones.

Instructions: Light the pink candle, hold the Citrine, and visualize harmony and love radiating through your relationships.

Stress Relief Spell

Purpose: To relieve stress and tension.

Materials: Citrine, blue candle, calming music.

Instructions: Light the blue candle, hold the Citrine, and listen to calming music while visualizing stress leaving your body.

Self-Empowerment Spell

Purpose: To empower yourself with inner strength.

Materials: Citrine, yellow candle, mirror.

Instructions: Light the yellow candle, hold the Citrine, and look into the mirror, affirming your inner strength and capabilities.

Spiritual Growth Spell

Purpose: To enhance spiritual growth and wisdom.

Materials: Citrine, white candle, sacred space.

Instructions: Light the white candle, hold the Citrine, and meditate in your sacred space while seeking spiritual guidance and growth.

Protection for Home Spell

Purpose: To protect your home from negative energies.

Materials: Citrine, white candle, salt.

Instructions: Light the white candle, hold the Citrine, and sprinkle salt around your home while visualizing a protective shield.

Clarity of Mind Spell

Purpose: To achieve mental clarity and focus.

Materials: Citrine, purple candle.

Instructions: Light the purple candle, hold the Citrine, and clear your mind while focusing on clarity and understanding.

Emotional Healing Spell

Purpose: To heal emotional wounds and promote inner peace.

Materials: Citrine, pink candle, soothing crystals (such as Rose Quartz).

Instructions: Light the pink candle, hold the Citrine, and surround yourself with soothing crystals while visualizing emotional healing.

Manifestation of Dreams Spell

Purpose: To manifest your dreams and aspirations.

Materials: Citrine, green candle, dream journal.

Instructions: Light the green candle, hold the Citrine, and write down your dreams and aspirations in the dream journal while visualizing them coming true.

Positive Energy Infusion Spell

Purpose: To infuse your surroundings with positive energy.

Materials: Citrine, white candle, affirmations.

Instructions: Light the white candle, hold the Citrine, and recite affirmations while visualizing positivity radiating around you.

Career Advancement Spell

Purpose: To enhance career success and advancement.

Materials: Citrine, green candle, resume or career goals.

Instructions: Light the green candle, hold the Citrine, and focus on your career goals while visualizing success and advancement.

Self-Love Spell

Purpose: To enhance self-love and acceptance.

Materials: Citrine, pink candle, mirror.

Instructions: Light the pink candle, hold the Citrine, and look into the mirror, affirming love and acceptance for yourself.

Peaceful Sleep Spell

Purpose: To promote peaceful and restful sleep.

Materials: Citrine, blue candle, lavender sachet.

Instructions: Light the blue candle, hold the Citrine and lavender sachet, and place them near your bedside while visualizing a night of deep, restorative sleep.

Citrine is a stone of manifestation, abundance, and positivity. By integrating these spells into your practice, you can harness its energy to attract prosperity, promote self-confidence, and cleanse negative energies. Embrace the vibrant energy of Citrine and let it guide you towards a life filled with abundance and success. Each spell deepens your connection to this powerful crystal, enhancing your ability to manifest your desires and live your best life.

Tiger's Eye

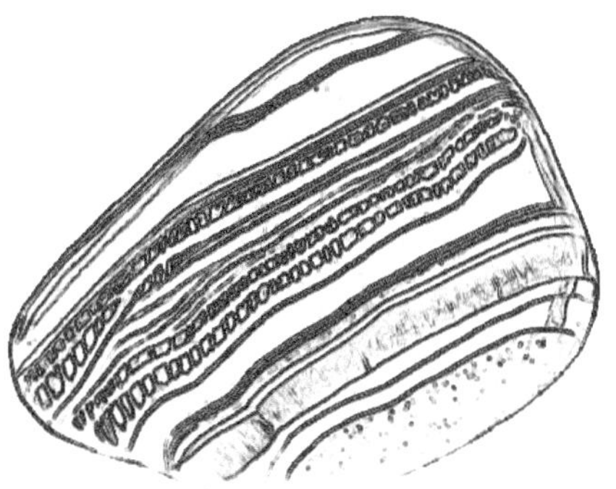

Introduction to Tiger's Eye

Tiger's Eye is a powerful stone known for its ability to bring good luck, protection, and courage. Its distinctive golden to red-brown coloration with chatoyant layers resembles the eye of a tiger, hence its name. This crystal has been prized throughout history for its grounding energy and its ability to empower the wearer with confidence and strength.

Properties and Uses of Tiger's Eye

Tiger's Eye is revered for its protective qualities, shielding the wearer from negative energies. It promotes mental clarity, focus, and courage, making it an ideal companion for those facing challenges or needing a boost of confidence. This stone is also associated with prosperity and luck, attracting abundance into the lives of those who embrace its energy.

Cleansing and Charging Tiger's Eye

To keep Tiger's Eye working at its best, cleanse it regularly using methods like running water, moonlight, or smudging with sage. Charging can be done under sunlight or with other crystals like Clear Quartz to amplify its energies.

Tiger's Eye Spells

Grounding and Stability Spell
Purpose: To promote grounding and stability.
Materials: Tiger's Eye, brown candle.
Instructions: Light the brown candle, hold the Tiger's Eye, and visualize roots extending from your body into the earth, grounding you deeply.

Courage and Confidence Spell
Purpose: To boost courage and self-confidence.
Materials: Tiger's Eye, yellow candle.
Instructions: Light the yellow candle, hold the Tiger's Eye, and affirm your courage and confidence in facing challenges.

Protection Spell
Purpose: To protect against negative energies.
Materials: Tiger's Eye, black candle.
Instructions: Light the black candle, hold the Tiger's Eye, and visualize a shield of protective light surrounding you.

Luck and Prosperity Spell
Purpose: To attract luck and prosperity.
Materials: Tiger's Eye, green candle.
Instructions: Light the green candle, hold the Tiger's Eye, and visualize opportunities for luck and prosperity coming your way.

Focus and Clarity Spell
Purpose: To enhance mental clarity and focus.
Materials: Tiger's Eye, white candle.
Instructions: Light the white candle, hold the Tiger's Eye, and visualize your mind becoming clear and focused on your goals.

Creativity and Inspiration Spell

Purpose: To enhance creativity and inspiration.
Materials: Tiger's Eye, orange candle.
Instructions: Light the orange candle, hold the Tiger's Eye, and engage in creative activities while allowing inspiration to flow.

Emotional Stability Spell

Purpose: To achieve emotional balance.
Materials: Tiger's Eye, pink candle.
Instructions: Light the pink candle, hold the Tiger's Eye, and visualize emotional stability and inner peace.

Intuition Enhancement Spell

Purpose: To enhance intuition and inner wisdom.
Materials: Tiger's Eye, indigo candle.
Instructions: Light the indigo candle, hold the Tiger's Eye, and meditate on opening your intuition to receive guidance.

Manifestation of Goals Spell

Purpose: To manifest your goals and desires.
Materials: Tiger's Eye, green candle.
Instructions: Light the green candle, hold the Tiger's Eye, and focus on your goals while visualizing them manifesting into reality.

Relationship Harmony Spell

Purpose: To promote harmony in relationships.
Materials: Tiger's Eye, pink candle, photo of loved ones.
Instructions: Light the pink candle, hold the Tiger's Eye, and visualize harmony and understanding in your relationships.

Health and Vitality Spell

Purpose: To enhance health and vitality.
Materials: Tiger's Eye, red candle.
Instructions: Light the red candle, hold the Tiger's Eye, and visualize vibrant energy filling your body.

Spiritual Protection Spell

Purpose: To protect spiritually against negative influences.
Materials: Tiger's Eye, white candle, sacred space.
Instructions: Light the white candle, hold the Tiger's Eye, and meditate in your sacred space while feeling spiritually protected.

Decision Making Spell

Purpose: To aid in making clear decisions.
Materials: Tiger's Eye, blue candle, list of options.
Instructions: Light the blue candle, hold the Tiger's Eye, and focus on gaining clarity and insight into your decisions.

Empowerment Spell

Purpose: To feel empowered and capable.
Materials: Tiger's Eye, gold candle, mirror.
Instructions: Light the gold candle, hold the Tiger's Eye, and look into the mirror, affirming your empowerment and capabilities.

Aura Cleansing Spell

Purpose: To cleanse and purify your aura.
Materials: Tiger's Eye, white candle, sage.
Instructions: Light the white candle, hold the Tiger's Eye, and burn sage while visualizing your aura being cleansed and purified.

Positive Outlook Spell

Purpose: To foster a positive outlook on life.
Materials: Tiger's Eye, yellow candle.
Instructions: Light the yellow candle, hold the Tiger's Eye, and visualize positivity and optimism surrounding you.

Success in Business Spell

Purpose: To attract success in business endeavors.
Materials: Tiger's Eye, green candle, business plan.
Instructions: Light the green candle, hold the Tiger's Eye, and visualize success and prosperity in your business ventures.

Enhanced Vitality Spell

Purpose: To enhance physical vitality.
Materials: Tiger's Eye, red candle, physical exercise.
Instructions: Light the red candle, hold the Tiger's Eye, and engage in physical exercise while feeling strong and vital.

Travel Protection Spell

Purpose: To protect during journeys.
Materials: Tiger's Eye, white candle, travel token.
Instructions: Light the white candle, hold the Tiger's Eye, and place the travel token near it while visualizing safe travels.

Creativity Flow Spell

Purpose: To enhance creative inspiration.
Materials: Tiger's Eye, orange candle, artistic tools.
Instructions: Light the orange candle, hold the Tiger's Eye, and engage in creative activities while feeling inspired.

Joy and Happiness Spell
Purpose: To attract joy and happiness into your life.
Materials: Tiger's Eye, yellow candle.
Instructions: Light the yellow candle, hold the Tiger's Eye, and focus on feelings of joy and happiness filling your heart.

Strength and Endurance Spell
Purpose: To enhance strength and endurance.
Materials: Tiger's Eye, red candle, exercise equipment.
Instructions: Light the red candle, hold the Tiger's Eye, and engage in physical exercise while feeling strong and enduring.

Manifestation of Goals Spell
Purpose: To manifest your goals and desires.
Materials: Tiger's Eye, green candle, list of goals.
Instructions: Light the green candle, hold the Tiger's Eye, and focus on your goals while visualizing them coming to fruition.

Spiritual Protection Spell
Purpose: To protect spiritually against negative influences.
Materials: Tiger's Eye, white candle, sacred space.
Instructions: Light the white candle, hold the Tiger's Eye, and meditate in your sacred space while feeling spiritually protected.

Tiger's Eye is a stone of courage, strength, and good fortune. Incorporating these spells into your practice can harness its energy for luck, protection, and empowerment. Embrace the strength of Tiger's Eye and allow it to guide you confidently through life's challenges. Each spell deepens your connection to this powerful crystal, enhancing your ability to manifest positivity and achieve success.

Selenite

Introduction to Selenite

Selenite is a crystal known for its high vibration and ability to cleanse, purify, and charge other crystals. Its name derives from the Greek goddess of the moon, Selene, reflecting its association with lunar energy. This translucent white crystal has a gentle yet powerful energy that brings peace, clarity, and spiritual growth to those who work with it.

Properties and Uses of Selenite

Selenite is prized for its purifying and cleansing properties. It has the unique ability to quickly unblock stagnant energy and remove negative energies. This crystal also enhances mental clarity, improves focus, and promotes a deep sense of inner peace. It is often used to create a peaceful atmosphere and facilitate meditation.

Cleansing and Charging Selenite

To keep Selenite clear and charged, place it on a selenite charging plate, or expose it to moonlight. Its self-cleansing properties make it ideal for purifying other crystals and spaces. Avoid using water to cleanse Selenite as it can degrade over time.

Selenite Spells

Purification Spell

Purpose: To purify and cleanse your space.

Materials: Selenite, white candle.

Instructions: Light the white candle, hold the Selenite, and move it around your space, visualizing negative energies being replaced with pure, positive energy.

Clarity of Mind Spell

Purpose: To enhance mental clarity and focus.

Materials: Selenite, blue candle.

Instructions: Light the blue candle, hold the Selenite, and meditate while focusing on clarity of thought and understanding.

Peace and Serenity Spell

Purpose: To promote peace and tranquility.

Materials: Selenite, pink candle.

Instructions: Light the pink candle, hold the Selenite, and visualize a calm and peaceful environment surrounding you.

Spiritual Guidance Spell

Purpose: To connect with spiritual guides.

Materials: Selenite, purple candle.

Instructions: Light the purple candle, hold the Selenite, and meditate while seeking guidance and wisdom from your spiritual guides.

Energy Clearing Spell

Purpose: To clear negative energy from your aura.

Materials: Selenite, sage bundle, white candle.

Instructions: Light the white candle, burn the sage, and pass the Selenite through the smoke while visualizing your aura being cleansed and purified.

Healing Light Spell

Purpose: To promote physical and emotional healing.

Materials: Selenite, green candle, healing crystals.

Instructions: Light the green candle, hold the Selenite, and surround yourself with healing crystals while visualizing healing light entering your body and spirit.

Protection from Psychic Attack Spell

Purpose: To protect against negative psychic energies.

Materials: Selenite, black candle.

Instructions: Light the black candle, hold the Selenite, and visualize a shield of protective light surrounding your mind and spirit.

Dream Recall Spell

Purpose: To enhance dream recall and interpretation.

Materials: Selenite, purple candle, dream journal.

Instructions: Light the purple candle, hold the Selenite, and write down your dreams in the dream journal upon waking while focusing on recall and interpretation.

Serenity at Home Spell

Purpose: To create a peaceful atmosphere at home.

Materials: Selenite, white candle, incense.

Instructions: Light the white candle, hold the Selenite, and burn incense while visualizing your home filled with serenity and tranquility.

Emotional Healing Spell

Purpose: To heal emotional wounds and promote inner peace.

Materials: Selenite, pink candle, soothing music.

Instructions: Light the pink candle, hold the Selenite, and listen to soothing music while visualizing emotional wounds healing and inner peace growing.

Protection during Meditation Spell

Purpose: To protect during meditation.

Materials: Selenite, white candle, meditation cushion.

Instructions: Light the white candle, hold the Selenite, and sit on your meditation cushion while meditating on protection and safety.

Connection with Higher Self Spell

Purpose: To strengthen your connection with your higher self.

Materials: Selenite, blue candle, quiet space.

Instructions: Light the blue candle, hold the Selenite, and meditate in your quiet space while focusing on connecting with your higher self.

Spiritual Awakening Spell

Purpose: To awaken spiritual awareness.

Materials: Selenite, white candle, meditation cushion.

Instructions: Light the white candle, hold the Selenite, and sit on your meditation cushion while meditating on awakening your spiritual awareness.

Aura Cleansing Spell

Purpose: To cleanse and brighten your aura.

Materials: Selenite, white candle, lavender oil.

Instructions: Light the white candle, hold the Selenite, and anoint yourself with lavender oil while visualizing your aura being cleansed and brightened.

Chakra Balancing Spell

Purpose: To balance and align your chakras.

Materials: Selenite, rainbow-colored candles.

Instructions: Light the rainbow-colored candles, hold the Selenite, and meditate on each chakra being balanced and aligned.

Enhanced Intuition Spell

Purpose: To enhance intuitive abilities.

Materials: Selenite, indigo candle.

Instructions: Light the indigo candle, hold the Selenite, and focus on enhancing your intuitive abilities during meditation.

Inner Peace Spell

Purpose: To cultivate inner peace.

Materials: Selenite, green candle.

Instructions: Light the green candle, hold the Selenite, and meditate on cultivating inner peace and harmony within yourself.

Meditation Enhancement Spell

Purpose: To enhance the meditation experience.

Materials: Selenite, white candle, meditation cushion.

Instructions: Light the white candle, hold the Selenite, and sit on your meditation cushion while focusing on deepening your meditation experience.

Energy Shield Spell

Purpose: To create an energy shield for protection.

Materials: Selenite, white candle.

Instructions: Light the white candle, hold the Selenite, and visualize an energy shield forming around you for protection.

Stress Relief Spell

Purpose: To relieve stress and promote relaxation.

Materials: Selenite, blue candle, calming music.

Instructions: Light the blue candle, hold the Selenite, and listen to calming music while visualizing stress melting away.

Spiritual Growth Spell

Purpose: To promote spiritual growth and development.

Materials: Selenite, purple candle, meditation cushion.

Instructions: Light the purple candle, hold the Selenite, and sit on your meditation cushion while focusing on spiritual growth and development.

Positive Energy Spell

Purpose: To attract positive energy.

Materials: Selenite, yellow candle.

Instructions: Light the yellow candle, hold the Selenite, and visualize positive energy flowing into your life.

Calmness and Relaxation Spell

Purpose: To promote calmness and relaxation.

Materials: Selenite, lavender candle.

Instructions: Light the lavender candle, hold the Selenite, and visualize calmness and relaxation filling your mind and body.

Self-Discovery Spell

Purpose: To aid in self-discovery and understanding.

Materials: Selenite, white candle, journal.

Instructions: Light the white candle, hold the Selenite, and journal about your inner thoughts and discoveries.

Spiritual Cleansing Spell

Purpose: To cleanse the spirit of negative influences.

Materials: Selenite, white candle, sage bundle.

Instructions: Light the white candle, burn the sage, and pass the Selenite through the smoke while visualizing your spirit being cleansed of negative influences.

Selenite is a crystal of purification, clarity, and spiritual growth. By incorporating these spells into your practice, you can harness its energy to cleanse negativity, enhance clarity of mind, and promote inner peace. Embrace the serene energy of Selenite and allow it to guide you on your spiritual journey. Each spell deepens your connection to this powerful crystal, enriching your spiritual practice and bringing harmony to your life.

Hematite

Introduction to Hematite

Hematite is a grounding stone known for its protective and stabilizing properties. Its name is derived from the Greek word "haima," meaning blood, due to the reddish-brown streaks often found on its surface. This shiny, metallic crystal has been used for centuries for its ability to absorb negative energy and promote a strong connection with the Earth.

Properties and Uses of Hematite

Hematite is highly effective for grounding and protecting. It harmonizes the mind, body, and spirit, promoting feelings of safety and security. This crystal also enhances willpower, courage, and confidence, making it beneficial for those seeking stability and strength in challenging situations. It is often used to balance the root chakra and facilitate energy flow throughout the body.

Cleansing and Charging Hematite

To cleanse Hematite, place it on a bed of hematite stones or visualize it being cleansed by white light. Avoid using water as it can cause it to rust. Charging Hematite can be done by placing it on a clear quartz cluster or exposing it to moonlight.

Hematite Spells

Grounding and Stability Spell

Purpose: To ground yourself and promote stability.

Materials: Hematite, black candle, earth element (soil or rock).

Instructions: Light the black candle, hold the Hematite, and sit with your feet on the earth element, focusing on grounding and stability.

Protection Shield Spell

Purpose: To create a protective shield around you.

Materials: Hematite, white candle.

Instructions: Light the white candle, hold the Hematite, and visualize a strong protective shield forming around your aura.

Strength and Courage Spell

Purpose: To boost inner strength and courage.

Materials: Hematite, red candle.

Instructions: Light the red candle, hold the Hematite, and affirm your strength and courage in facing challenges.

Energy Balancing Spell

Purpose: To balance your energy centers (chakras).

Materials: Hematite, rainbow candle (or seven different colored candles representing the chakras).

Instructions: Light each candle representing the chakras, hold the Hematite, and visualize each energy center aligning and balancing.

Confidence Boost Spell

Purpose: To enhance self-confidence.

Materials: Hematite, yellow candle, mirror.

Instructions: Light the yellow candle, hold the Hematite, and look into the mirror, affirming your confidence and self-worth.

Decision-Making Clarity Spell

Purpose: To gain clarity in decision-making.

Materials: Hematite, blue candle, list of options.

Instructions: Light the blue candle, hold the Hematite, and meditate while focusing on gaining clarity and insight into your decisions.

Stress Relief Spell

Purpose: To alleviate stress and tension.

Materials: Hematite, lavender candle, calming essential oils.

Instructions: Light the lavender candle, hold the Hematite, and inhale the calming scent while visualizing stress leaving your body.

Empowerment Spell

Purpose: To feel empowered and in control.

Materials: Hematite, orange candle.

Instructions: Light the orange candle, hold the Hematite, and visualize the energy of the crystal empowering you in all aspects of your life.

Physical Healing Spell

Purpose: To promote physical healing.

Materials: Hematite, green candle, healing herbs.

Instructions: Light the green candle, hold the Hematite, and visualize healing energy flowing through your body.

Patience and Endurance Spell

Purpose: To cultivate patience and endurance.

Materials: Hematite, purple candle.

Instructions: Light the purple candle, hold the Hematite, and meditate while focusing on patience and endurance in challenging times.

Focus and Concentration Spell

Purpose: To improve focus and mental clarity.

Materials: Hematite, yellow candle.

Instructions: Light the yellow candle, hold the Hematite, and focus on clear and focused thoughts.

Emotional Stability Spell

Purpose: To achieve emotional balance and stability.

Materials: Hematite, blue candle, calming music.

Instructions: Light the blue candle, hold the Hematite, and play calming music while visualizing emotional stability.

Protection from Negative Energies Spell

Purpose: To shield against negative energies.

Materials: Hematite, black candle.

Instructions: Light the black candle, hold the Hematite, and visualize it forming a protective barrier around you.

Career Success Spell

Purpose: To enhance career success and advancement.

Materials: Hematite, green candle, professional goals.

Instructions: Light the green candle, hold the Hematite, and focus on your career aspirations while visualizing success and achievement.

Restful Sleep Spell

Purpose: To promote restful and rejuvenating sleep.

Materials: Hematite, blue candle, calming crystals (such as Amethyst).

Instructions: Light the blue candle, hold the Hematite, and place calming crystals near your bedside while visualizing a night of deep, restorative sleep.

Grounding Meditation Spell

Purpose: To deepen grounding during meditation.

Materials: Hematite, brown candle, meditation cushion.

Instructions: Light the brown candle, hold the Hematite, and sit on your meditation cushion while focusing on grounding energy connecting you to the earth.

Manifestation Spell

Purpose: To aid in manifesting desires.

Materials: Hematite, gold candle, written intention.

Instructions: Light the gold candle, hold the Hematite, and read your written intention out loud while visualizing it coming to fruition.

Root Chakra Activation Spell

Purpose: To activate and balance the root chakra.

Materials: Hematite, red candle, grounding essential oils (such as patchouli or cedarwood).

Instructions: Light the red candle, hold the Hematite, and anoint yourself with grounding essential oils while focusing on activating your root chakra.

Courageous Heart Spell

Purpose: To boost courage and bravery.

Materials: Hematite, orange candle, heart-shaped object.

Instructions: Light the orange candle, hold the Hematite, and place the heart-shaped object in front of you while focusing on increasing your courage and bravery.

Energy Cleansing Spell

Purpose: To cleanse and purify personal energy.

Materials: Hematite, sage bundle, white candle.

Instructions: Light the white candle, burn the sage, and pass the Hematite through the smoke while visualizing your personal energy being cleansed and purified.

Endurance and Stamina Spell

Purpose: To enhance physical endurance and stamina.

Materials: Hematite, red candle, motivational music.

Instructions: Light the red candle, hold the Hematite, and listen to motivational music while visualizing increased endurance and stamina.

Safety and Security Spell

Purpose: To enhance feelings of safety and security.

Materials: Hematite, black candle, protective talisman.

Instructions: Light the black candle, hold the Hematite, and place the protective talisman near you while focusing on feelings of safety and security.

Positive Transformation Spell

Purpose: To encourage positive transformation.

Materials: Hematite, green candle, butterfly symbol.

Instructions: Light the green candle, hold the Hematite, and visualize positive transformation in your life while focusing on the butterfly symbol.

Emotional Healing Spell

Purpose: To heal emotional wounds.

Materials: Hematite, pink candle, rose quartz.

Instructions: Light the pink candle, hold the Hematite, and place the rose quartz near you while visualizing emotional healing.

Personal Power Spell

Purpose: To enhance personal power and self-assurance.

Materials: Hematite, yellow candle, tiger's eye crystal.

Instructions: Light the yellow candle, hold the Hematite, and place the tiger's eye crystal near you while focusing on enhancing your personal power and self-assurance.

Hematite is a powerful crystal for grounding, protection, and strength. By incorporating these spells into your practice, you can harness its energy to achieve stability, boost confidence, and balance your energy centers. Embrace the protective and grounding qualities of Hematite as you work with it in your spiritual and personal journey. Each spell deepens your connection to this resilient crystal, empowering you to navigate challenges with strength and courage.

Lapis Lazuli

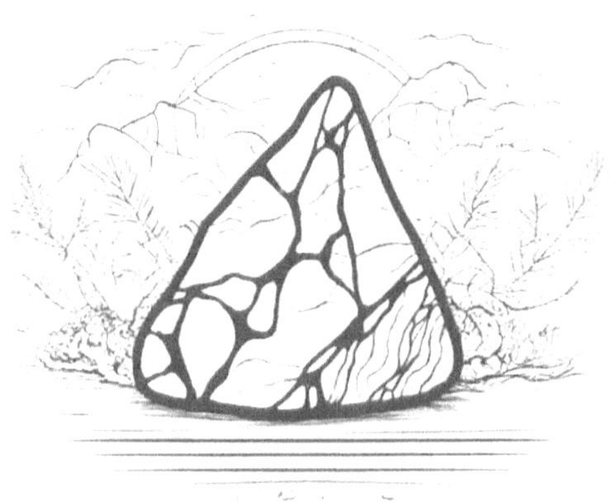

Introduction to Lapis Lazuli

Lapis Lazuli is a deep blue stone with golden flecks of pyrite, symbolizing royalty and honor. It has been revered for centuries for its connection to wisdom, intuition, and spiritual enlightenment. Used by ancient civilizations for its powerful metaphysical properties, Lapis Lazuli remains highly regarded for enhancing intellectual abilities and spiritual awareness.

Properties and Uses of Lapis Lazuli

Lapis Lazuli is a stone of truth and wisdom, encouraging honesty of the spirit and clarity of thought. It activates the higher mind, enhancing intellectual abilities and stimulating the desire for knowledge, truth, and understanding. This crystal also promotes self-awareness, inner peace, and harmony within relationships.

Cleansing and Charging Lapis Lazuli

To cleanse Lapis Lazuli, place it on a bed of hematite stones or cleanse it with sage smoke. Avoid using water as it can damage the stone. Charging Lapis Lazuli can be done by placing it on an amethyst cluster or under the light of the full moon.

Lapis Lazuli Spells

Wisdom and Clarity Spell

Purpose: To enhance wisdom and clarity.

Materials: Lapis Lazuli, white candle.

Instructions: Light the white candle, hold the Lapis Lazuli, and meditate while seeking wisdom and clarity on a specific issue or question.

Intuition Enhancement Spell

Purpose: To strengthen intuition.

Materials: Lapis Lazuli, purple candle.

Instructions: Light the purple candle, hold the Lapis Lazuli, and meditate while focusing on enhancing your intuitive abilities.

Truth and Communication Spell

Purpose: To promote truthful communication.

Materials: Lapis Lazuli, blue candle.

Instructions: Light the blue candle, hold the Lapis Lazuli, and communicate openly and honestly while holding the crystal.

Self-Awareness Spell

Purpose: To enhance self-awareness.

Materials: Lapis Lazuli, mirror.

Instructions: Look into the mirror while holding the Lapis Lazuli and reflect on your strengths, weaknesses, and areas for personal growth.

Emotional Healing Spell

Purpose: To heal emotional wounds.

Materials: Lapis Lazuli, pink candle, soothing music.

Instructions: Light the pink candle, hold the Lapis Lazuli, and listen to soothing music while visualizing emotional wounds healing and inner peace growing.

Spiritual Enlightenment Spell

Purpose: To achieve spiritual enlightenment.

Materials: Lapis Lazuli, gold candle.

Instructions: Light the gold candle, hold the Lapis Lazuli, and meditate while focusing on connecting with higher spiritual realms.

Enhanced Memory Spell

Purpose: To improve memory.

Materials: Lapis Lazuli, yellow candle.

Instructions: Light the yellow candle, hold the Lapis Lazuli, and meditate while focusing on improving your memory and mental recall.

Inner Peace Spell

Purpose: To promote inner peace and harmony.

Materials: Lapis Lazuli, green candle.

Instructions: Light the green candle, hold the Lapis Lazuli, and meditate while visualizing a sense of calm and tranquility filling your being.

Creativity Boost Spell

Purpose: To enhance creativity.

Materials: Lapis Lazuli, orange candle, artistic materials.

Instructions: Light the orange candle, hold the Lapis Lazuli, and engage in artistic activities while allowing creativity to flow.

Psychic Abilities Spell

Purpose: To enhance psychic abilities.

Materials: Lapis Lazuli, indigo candle.

Instructions: Light the indigo candle, hold the Lapis Lazuli, and meditate while focusing on developing your psychic senses.

Harmonious Relationships Spell

Purpose: To promote harmony in relationships.

Materials: Lapis Lazuli, pink candle, photo of loved ones.

Instructions: Light the pink candle, hold the Lapis Lazuli, and focus on sending love and harmony to your relationships.

Protection from Negative Energies Spell

Purpose: To shield against negative energies.

Materials: Lapis Lazuli, black candle.

Instructions: Light the black candle, hold the Lapis Lazuli, and visualize it forming a protective shield around you.

Inspiration Spell

Purpose: To attract inspiration.

Materials: Lapis Lazuli, white candle, writing materials.

Instructions: Light the white candle, hold the Lapis Lazuli, and write down your inspirations and ideas while focusing on creativity.

Confidence Spell

Purpose: To boost self-confidence.

Materials: Lapis Lazuli, yellow candle, mirror.

Instructions: Light the yellow candle, hold the Lapis Lazuli, and look into the mirror while affirming your self-worth and confidence.

Focus and Concentration Spell

Purpose: To improve focus and mental clarity.

Materials: Lapis Lazuli, yellow candle.

Instructions: Light the yellow candle, hold the Lapis Lazuli, and focus on clear and focused thoughts.

Self-Expression Spell

Purpose: To enhance self-expression.

Materials: Lapis Lazuli, blue candle, journal.

Instructions: Light the blue candle, hold the Lapis Lazuli, and write in your journal, expressing your thoughts and feelings freely.

Manifestation of Desires Spell

Purpose: To manifest your desires and intentions.

Materials: Lapis Lazuli, white candle, written desires.

Instructions: Light the white candle, hold the Lapis Lazuli, and focus on your desires and intentions while visualizing them coming to fruition.

Financial Growth Spell

Purpose: To promote financial growth and stability.

Materials: Lapis Lazuli, gold candle, financial documents.

Instructions: Light the gold candle, hold the Lapis Lazuli, and focus on your financial growth and stability. Visualize your finances increasing and becoming more stable over time.

Protection Spell

Purpose: To protect yourself from harm.

Materials: Lapis Lazuli, black candle.

Instructions: Light the black candle, hold the Lapis Lazuli, and visualize a protective shield surrounding you, keeping you safe from harm.

Love Attraction Spell

Purpose: To attract love into your life.

Materials: Lapis Lazuli, pink candle, rose petals.

Instructions: Light the pink candle, hold the Lapis Lazuli, and visualize love and romance entering your life.

Healing and Recovery Spell

Purpose: To promote healing and recovery from illness or injury.

Materials: Lapis Lazuli, green candle, healing herbs.

Instructions: Light the green candle, hold the Lapis Lazuli, and visualize healing energy flowing through your body.

New Beginnings Spell

Purpose: To attract new beginnings and fresh starts.

Materials: Lapis Lazuli, white candle.

Instructions: Light the white candle, hold the Lapis Lazuli, and visualize new opportunities and fresh starts coming into your life.

Success and Achievement Spell

Purpose: To enhance success and achievement.

Materials: Lapis Lazuli, gold candle.

Instructions: Light the gold candle, hold the Lapis Lazuli, and visualize yourself achieving your goals and succeeding in your endeavors.

Stress Relief Spell

Purpose: To alleviate stress and promote relaxation.

Materials: Lapis Lazuli, lavender candle, calming essential oils.

Instructions: Light the lavender candle, hold the Lapis Lazuli, and inhale the calming scent while visualizing stress leaving your body.

Abundance Attraction Spell

Purpose: To attract abundance in all forms.

Materials: Lapis Lazuli, green candle, symbols of abundance.

Instructions: Light the green candle, hold the Lapis Lazuli, and visualize abundance flowing into your life from all directions.

Inner Strength Spell

Purpose: To enhance inner strength and resilience.

Materials: Lapis Lazuli, red candle.

Instructions: Light the red candle, hold the Lapis Lazuli, and affirm your inner strength and resilience in overcoming challenges.

Lapis Lazuli is a stone of wisdom, truth, and spiritual awareness. By incorporating these spells into your practice, you can harness its energy to enhance intuition, promote truthful communication, and achieve inner peace. Embrace the deep blue hues and golden flecks of Lapis Lazuli as you connect with its transformative energy. Each spell deepens your connection to this ancient crystal, guiding you on a path of wisdom and enlightenment.

Carnelian

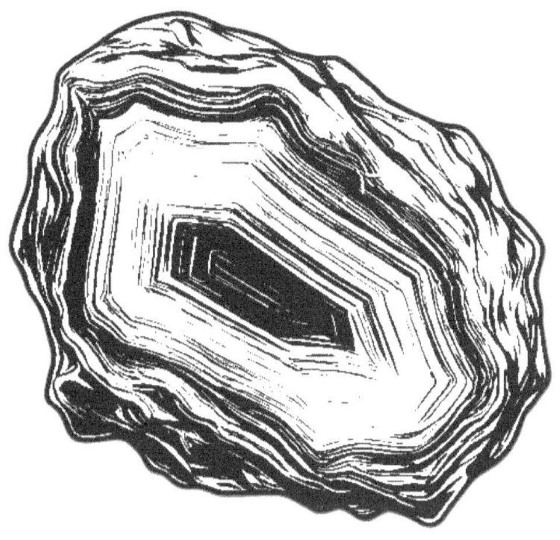

Introduction to Carnelian

Carnelian is a vibrant orange-red crystal known for its warm and energizing properties. It has been prized throughout history for its association with courage, vitality, and creativity. This translucent stone ranges in color from pale orange to deep red and is often used to boost confidence, creativity, and passion.

Properties and Uses of Carnelian

Carnelian is a crystal of motivation and endurance, stimulating ambition and drive. It promotes courage, confidence, and self-expression, making it ideal for those seeking to take bold actions and pursue their goals with determination. This crystal also enhances creativity, vitality, and passion for life.

Cleansing and Charging Carnelian

To cleanse Carnelian, place it under running water or cleanse it with sage smoke. Charging Carnelian can be done by placing it on a quartz cluster or under the light of the sun. Its vibrant energy responds well to sunlight, revitalizing its properties.

<u>Carnelian Spells</u>

Confidence Boost Spell

Purpose: To boost self-confidence.

Materials: Carnelian, yellow candle, mirror.

Instructions: Light the yellow candle, hold the Carnelian, and look into the mirror while affirming your self-worth and confidence.

Creativity Spell

Purpose: To enhance creativity.

Materials: Carnelian, orange candle, artistic materials.

Instructions: Light the orange candle, hold the Carnelian, and engage in creative activities while allowing inspiration to flow.

Motivation Spell

Purpose: To increase motivation and drive.

Materials: Carnelian, red candle.

Instructions: Light the red candle, hold the Carnelian, and visualize yourself achieving your goals with determination and perseverance.

Passion Spell

Purpose: To ignite passion and enthusiasm.

Materials: Carnelian, pink candle.

Instructions: Light the pink candle, hold the Carnelian, and meditate while focusing on what brings passion and joy into your life.

Courage Spell

Purpose: To boost courage and strength.

Materials: Carnelian, blue candle.

Instructions: Light the blue candle, hold the Carnelian, and affirm your courage in facing challenges and overcoming obstacles.

Vitality Spell

Purpose: To enhance vitality and energy levels.

Materials: Carnelian, green candle.

Instructions: Light the green candle, hold the Carnelian, and visualize vibrant energy flowing through your body.

Action and Initiative Spell

Purpose: To take decisive action and initiative.

Materials: Carnelian, white candle.

Instructions: Light the white candle, hold the Carnelian, and focus on taking proactive steps towards your goals.

Self-Expression Spell

Purpose: To enhance self-expression.

Materials: Carnelian, purple candle.

Instructions: Light the purple candle, hold the Carnelian, and express yourself creatively through writing, art, or speaking.

Emotional Healing Spell

Purpose: To heal emotional wounds and promote emotional balance.

Materials: Carnelian, pink candle, soothing music.

Instructions: Light the pink candle, hold the Carnelian, and listen to soothing music while visualizing emotional wounds healing.

Success in Business Spell

Purpose: To attract success in business endeavors.

Materials: Carnelian, green candle, business plan.

Instructions: Light the green candle, hold the Carnelian, and visualize success and prosperity in your business ventures.

Joy and Happiness Spell

Purpose: To attract joy and happiness into your life.

Materials: Carnelian, yellow candle.

Instructions: Light the yellow candle, hold the Carnelian, and focus on feelings of joy and happiness filling your heart.

Protection from Negative Energy Spell

Purpose: To shield against negative energy.

Materials: Carnelian, black candle.

Instructions: Light the black candle, hold the Carnelian, and visualize it forming a protective shield around you.

Enhanced Vitality and Stamina Spell

Purpose: To enhance physical vitality and stamina.

Materials: Carnelian, red candle, physical exercise.

Instructions: Light the red candle, hold the Carnelian, and engage in physical exercise while visualizing increased vitality.

Manifestation of Goals Spell

Purpose: To manifest your goals into reality.

Materials: Carnelian, green candle, written goals.

Instructions: Light the green candle, hold the Carnelian, and focus on your goals while visualizing them coming to fruition.

Creative Problem-Solving Spell

Purpose: To find creative solutions to problems.

Materials: Carnelian, yellow candle, notebook.

Instructions: Light the yellow candle, hold the Carnelian, and brainstorm creative solutions while writing them in the notebook.

Grounding and Stability Spell

Purpose: To promote grounding and stability.

Materials: Carnelian, brown candle.

Instructions: Light the brown candle, hold the Carnelian, and meditate while visualizing a deep connection to the earth and feeling grounded.

Social Confidence Spell

Purpose: To boost confidence in social situations.

Materials: Carnelian, blue candle, social gathering.

Instructions: Light the blue candle, hold the Carnelian, and visualize yourself feeling confident and comfortable in social settings.

Sexual Energy Spell

Purpose: To enhance sexual energy and passion.

Materials: Carnelian, red candle.

Instructions: Light the red candle, hold the Carnelian, and focus on increasing your sexual energy and passion.

Creativity in Writing Spell

Purpose: To enhance creativity in writing.

Materials: Carnelian, orange candle, writing materials.

Instructions: Light the orange candle, hold the Carnelian, and begin writing, allowing creativity to flow through you.

Fear Release Spell

Purpose: To release fears and anxieties.

Materials: Carnelian, black candle.

Instructions: Light the black candle, hold the Carnelian, and visualize releasing fears and anxieties, allowing courage to take their place.

Enhanced Physical Performance Spell

Purpose: To boost physical performance.

Materials: Carnelian, red candle, workout gear.

Instructions: Light the red candle, hold the Carnelian, and focus on enhancing your physical performance while engaging in exercise.

Public Speaking Confidence Spell

Purpose: To gain confidence in public speaking.

Materials: Carnelian, yellow candle, speech notes.

Instructions: Light the yellow candle, hold the Carnelian, and practice your speech while visualizing confidence and clarity in your delivery.

Passion for Life Spell

Purpose: To reignite passion and zest for life.

Materials: Carnelian, pink candle.

Instructions: Light the pink candle, hold the Carnelian, and meditate on the things that bring you joy and enthusiasm for life.

Overcoming Procrastination Spell

Purpose: To overcome procrastination and take action.

Materials: Carnelian, red candle, to-do list.

Instructions: Light the red candle, hold the Carnelian, and focus on completing tasks on your to-do list with energy and determination.

Artistic Inspiration Spell

Purpose: To inspire artistic creativity.

Materials: Carnelian, orange candle, art supplies.

Instructions: Light the orange candle, hold the Carnelian, and engage in your artistic practice, allowing inspiration to guide your creations.

Carnelian is a crystal of vitality, creativity, and courage. By incorporating these spells into your practice, you can harness its energy to boost confidence, enhance creativity, and ignite passion in your pursuits. Embrace the vibrant energy of Carnelian as you work towards achieving your goals and expressing your true self. Each spell deepens your connection to this dynamic crystal, empowering you to live life with courage and enthusiasm.

Aventurine

Introduction to Aventurine

Aventurine is a stone of luck and abundance, known for its soothing and calming energies. This translucent quartz comes in shades of green, often with shimmering metallic flecks, which give it a sparkling appearance. *Aventurine* has been used throughout history for its ability to attract prosperity, opportunity, and good fortune.

Properties and Uses of Aventurine

Aventurine is a stone of opportunity and optimism, encouraging luck, prosperity, and growth in all aspects of life. It promotes a sense of well-being and emotional calm, making it ideal for those seeking balance and harmony. This crystal also enhances creativity, decisiveness, and leadership qualities.

Cleansing and Charging Aventurine

To cleanse *Aventurine*, place it under running water or cleanse it with sage smoke. Charging *Aventurine* can be done by placing it on a quartz cluster or under the light of the full moon. Its soothing energy responds well to natural elements, revitalizing its properties.

Aventurine Spells

Luck and Prosperity Spell

Purpose: To attract luck and prosperity.

Materials: Aventurine, green candle, coins or symbols of prosperity.

Instructions: Light the green candle, hold the Aventurine, and visualize opportunities and abundance flowing into your life.

Emotional Healing Spell

Purpose: To heal emotional wounds and promote emotional balance.

Materials: Aventurine, pink candle, soothing music.

Instructions: Light the pink candle, hold the Aventurine, and listen to soothing music while visualizing emotional wounds healing.

Decision-Making Spell

Purpose: To make clear and confident decisions.

Materials: Aventurine, blue candle, list of options.

Instructions: Light the blue candle, hold the Aventurine, and meditate while focusing on gaining clarity and confidence in your decisions.

Harmony and Balance Spell

Purpose: To promote harmony and balance in life.

Materials: Aventurine, white candle.

Instructions: Light the white candle, hold the Aventurine, and meditate while visualizing a balanced and harmonious life.

Creativity Boost Spell

Purpose: To enhance creativity.

Materials: Aventurine, orange candle, artistic materials.

Instructions: Light the orange candle, hold the Aventurine, and engage in creative activities while allowing inspiration to flow.

Heart Chakra Healing Spell

Purpose: To heal and balance the heart chakra.

Materials: Aventurine, green candle.

Instructions: Light the green candle, hold the Aventurine, and meditate while focusing on healing and balancing your heart chakra.

Self-Confidence Spell

Purpose: To boost self-confidence.

Materials: Aventurine, yellow candle, mirror.

Instructions: Light the yellow candle, hold the Aventurine, and look into the mirror while affirming your self-worth and confidence.

Prosperity in Business Spell

Purpose: To attract prosperity in business endeavors.

Materials: Aventurine, green candle, business plan.

Instructions: Light the green candle, hold the Aventurine, and visualize success and prosperity in your business ventures.

Peaceful Sleep Spell

Purpose: To promote restful and rejuvenating sleep.

Materials: Aventurine, blue candle, calming crystals (such as Amethyst).

Instructions: Light the blue candle, hold the Aventurine, and place calming crystals near your bedside while visualizing a night of deep, restorative sleep.

Protection from Negative Energies Spell

Purpose: To shield against negative energies.

Materials: Aventurine, black candle.

Instructions: Light the black candle, hold the Aventurine, and visualize it forming a protective shield around you.

Optimism and Joy Spell

Purpose: To attract optimism and joy into your life.

Materials: Aventurine, yellow candle.

Instructions: Light the yellow candle, hold the Aventurine, and focus on feelings of optimism and joy filling your heart.

Confidence in Relationships Spell

Purpose: To boost confidence in relationships.

Materials: Aventurine, pink candle, photo of loved ones.

Instructions: Light the pink candle, hold the Aventurine, and focus on sending love and confidence to your relationships.

Success and Achievement Spell

Purpose: To enhance success and achievement.

Materials: Aventurine, gold candle.

Instructions: Light the gold candle, hold the Aventurine, and visualize yourself achieving your goals and succeeding in your endeavors.

Stress Relief Spell

Purpose: To alleviate stress and promote relaxation.

Materials: Aventurine, lavender candle, calming essential oils.

Instructions: Light the lavender candle, hold the Aventurine, and inhale the calming scent while visualizing stress leaving your body.

Abundance Attraction Spell

Purpose: To attract abundance in all forms.

Materials: Aventurine, green candle, symbols of abundance (e.g., coins, leaves).

Instructions: Light the green candle, hold the Aventurine, and visualize abundance flowing into your life from all directions.

Inner Strength Spell

Purpose: To enhance inner strength and resilience.

Materials: Aventurine, red candle.

Instructions: Light the red candle, hold the Aventurine, and affirm your inner strength and resilience in overcoming challenges.

Focus and Concentration Spell

Purpose: To improve focus and mental clarity.

Materials: Aventurine, yellow candle.

Instructions: Light the yellow candle, hold the Aventurine, and focus on clear and focused thoughts.

Health and Wellness Spell

Purpose: To promote overall health and wellness.

Materials: Aventurine, green candle, healing herbs.

Instructions: Light the green candle, hold the Aventurine, and visualize vibrant health and wellness flowing through your body.

Financial Growth Spell

Purpose: To promote financial growth and stability.

Materials: Aventurine, gold candle, financial documents (e.g., bank statements, investment plans).

Instructions: Light the gold candle, hold the Aventurine, and focus on your financial growth and stability. Visualize your finances increasing and becoming more stable over time.

Career Advancement Spell

Purpose: To enhance career advancement and opportunities.

Materials: Aventurine, green candle, resume or career goals.

Instructions: Light the green candle, hold the Aventurine, and visualize career advancement and opportunities opening up for you.

Spiritual Growth Spell

Purpose: To promote spiritual growth and enlightenment.

Materials: Aventurine, white candle.

Instructions: Light the white candle, hold the Aventurine, and meditate while focusing on your spiritual growth and connection to higher realms.

New Beginnings Spell

Purpose: To attract new beginnings and fresh starts.

Materials: Aventurine, white candle.

Instructions: Light the white candle, hold the Aventurine, and visualize new opportunities and fresh starts coming into your life.

Healing and Recovery Spell

Purpose: To promote healing and recovery from illness or injury.

Materials: Aventurine, green candle, healing crystals (e.g., Amethyst).

Instructions: Light the green candle, hold the Aventurine, and visualize healing energy flowing through your body.

Love and Compassion Spell

Purpose: To attract love and compassion into your life.

Materials: Aventurine, pink candle, rose petals.

Instructions: Light the pink candle, hold the Aventurine, and visualize love and compassion filling your heart and life.

Manifestation of Desires Spell

Purpose: To manifest your desires and intentions.

Materials: Aventurine, white candle, written desires.

Instructions: Light the white candle, hold the Aventurine, and focus on your desires and intentions while visualizing them coming to fruition.

Aventurine is a crystal of luck, abundance, and opportunity. By incorporating these spells into your practice, you can harness its energy to attract prosperity, enhance emotional balance, and promote creativity. Embrace the soothing green hues and shimmering qualities of Aventurine as you invite luck and positivity into your life. Each spell deepens your connection to this fortunate crystal, empowering you to manifest abundance and harmony in all aspects of your journey.

Labradorite

Introduction to Labradorite

Labradorite is a mesmerizing stone known for its iridescent flashes of color, ranging from blue and green to gold and purple. It is often referred to as the "Stone of Magic" due to its mystical properties that enhance intuition and psychic abilities. Labradorite is prized for its ability to protect against negativity and stimulate spiritual growth.

Properties and Uses of Labradorite

Labradorite is a stone of transformation and spiritual awakening, promoting psychic abilities, intuition, and spiritual insight. It is a powerful protector, shielding the aura from negative energies and enhancing one's ability to perceive the unseen. This crystal also encourages self-discovery, intuition development, and inner knowing.

Cleansing and Charging Labradorite

To cleanse Labradorite, pass it through sage smoke or place it on a bed of hematite stones. Avoid using water, as it can dull its iridescence. Charging Labradorite can be done under the light of the full moon or by placing it on a selenite charging plate to amplify its energies.

Labradorite Spells

Psychic Enhancement Spell

Purpose: To enhance psychic abilities.

Materials: Labradorite, indigo candle.

Instructions: Light the indigo candle, hold the Labradorite, and meditate while focusing on developing your psychic senses.

Aura Protection Spell

Purpose: To protect your aura.

Materials: Labradorite, purple candle.

Instructions: Light the purple candle, hold the Labradorite, and visualize a protective shield forming around your aura.

Intuition Development Spell

Purpose: To enhance intuition.

Materials: Labradorite, blue candle.

Instructions: Light the blue candle, hold the Labradorite, and meditate while focusing on enhancing your intuitive abilities.

Spiritual Awakening Spell

Purpose: To stimulate spiritual growth.

Materials: Labradorite, white candle.

Instructions: Light the white candle, hold the Labradorite, and meditate while focusing on spiritual insights and growth.

Protection from Negative Energies Spell

Purpose: To shield against negative energies.

Materials: Labradorite, black candle.

Instructions: Light the black candle, hold the Labradorite, and visualize it forming a protective barrier against negativity.

Manifestation Spell

Purpose: To manifest desires into reality.

Materials: Labradorite, green candle, manifestation journal.

Instructions: Light the green candle, hold the Labradorite, and write down your desires in the manifestation journal while visualizing them coming true.

Self-Discovery Spell

Purpose: To promote self-discovery.

Materials: Labradorite, yellow candle, journal.

Instructions: Light the yellow candle, hold the Labradorite, and journal about self-discovery and personal insights.

Clairvoyance Spell

Purpose: To enhance clairvoyant abilities.

Materials: Labradorite, violet candle.

Instructions: Light the violet candle, hold the Labradorite, and meditate while focusing on developing your clairvoyant skills.

Spirit Communication Spell

Purpose: To facilitate communication with spirits.

Materials: Labradorite, silver candle.

Instructions: Light the silver candle, hold the Labradorite, and meditate while focusing on connecting with spiritual energies.

Emotional Healing Spell

Purpose: To heal emotional wounds.

Materials: Labradorite, pink candle, calming crystals.

Instructions: Light the pink candle, hold the Labradorite, and place calming crystals around you while visualizing emotional healing.

Creativity Spell

Purpose: To enhance creativity.

Materials: Labradorite, orange candle, artistic materials.

Instructions: Light the orange candle, hold the Labradorite, and engage in creative activities while allowing inspiration to flow.

Dream Recall Spell

Purpose: To improve dream recall and interpretation.

Materials: Labradorite, white candle, dream journal.

Instructions: Light the white candle, hold the Labradorite, and keep your dream journal nearby. Before sleeping, focus on recalling and interpreting your dreams.

Transformation Spell

Purpose: To aid in personal transformation.

Materials: Labradorite, green candle, a small plant.

Instructions: Light the green candle, hold the Labradorite, and visualize your personal transformation while nurturing the small plant as a symbol of growth.

Courage and Strength Spell

Purpose: To enhance courage and strength.

Materials: Labradorite, red candle.

Instructions: Light the red candle, hold the Labradorite, and meditate while affirming your courage and inner strength.

Protection for Travelers Spell

Purpose: To ensure safe travels.

Materials: Labradorite, white candle, a map or travel itinerary.

Instructions: Light the white candle, hold the Labradorite, and visualize safe and protected travels while focusing on your destination.

Confidence Spell

Purpose: To boost self-confidence.

Materials: Labradorite, yellow candle, mirror.

Instructions: Light the yellow candle, hold the Labradorite, and look into the mirror while affirming your self-worth and confidence.

Enhanced Focus Spell

Purpose: To improve focus and concentration.

Materials: Labradorite, blue candle.

Instructions: Light the blue candle, hold the Labradorite, and meditate while focusing on clear and focused thoughts.

Stress Relief Spell

Purpose: To alleviate stress and promote relaxation.

Materials: Labradorite, lavender candle, calming essential oils.

Instructions: Light the lavender candle, hold the Labradorite, and inhale the calming scent while visualizing stress leaving your body.

Enhanced Communication Spell

Purpose: To improve communication skills.

Materials: Labradorite, blue candle, writing materials.

Instructions: Light the blue candle, hold the Labradorite, and focus on clear and effective communication while writing or speaking.

Harmony in Relationships Spell

Purpose: To promote harmony in relationships.

Materials: Labradorite, pink candle, photo of loved ones.

Instructions: Light the pink candle, hold the Labradorite, and focus on sending love and harmony to your relationships.

Healing the Heart Spell

Purpose: To heal emotional pain and heartbreak.

Materials: Labradorite, green candle.

Instructions: Light the green candle, hold the Labradorite, and meditate while focusing on healing your heart and releasing emotional pain.

Spiritual Protection Spell

Purpose: To protect against spiritual harm.

Materials: Labradorite, black candle.

Instructions: Light the black candle, hold the Labradorite, and visualize a protective shield surrounding you, keeping you safe from spiritual harm.

Enhanced Meditation Spell

Purpose: To deepen meditation practices.

Materials: Labradorite, white candle, meditation music.

Instructions: Light the white candle, hold the Labradorite, and meditate while listening to calming meditation music, focusing on deepening your practice.

Attracting Success Spell

Purpose: To attract success in your endeavors.

Materials: Labradorite, gold candle.

Instructions: Light the gold candle, hold the Labradorite, and visualize yourself achieving success in your goals and endeavors.

Balancing Emotions Spell

Purpose: To promote emotional balance.

Materials: Labradorite, blue candle.

Instructions: Light the blue candle, hold the Labradorite, and meditate while focusing on achieving emotional balance and harmony.

Past Life Recall Spell

Purpose: To recall past life experiences.

Materials: Labradorite, purple candle.

Instructions: Light the purple candle, hold the Labradorite, and meditate while focusing on recalling past life experiences and insights.

Labradorite is a stone of magic and transformation, revered for its mystical properties that enhance psychic abilities and spiritual insight. By incorporating these spells into your practice, you can harness its energy to protect your aura, enhance intuition, and stimulate spiritual growth. Embrace the iridescent beauty of Labradorite as you explore its transformative qualities. Each spell deepens your connection to this mystical crystal, guiding you on a path of spiritual awakening and intuitive discovery.

Smoky Quartz

Introduction to Smoky Quartz

Smoky Quartz is a powerful grounding and protective stone known for its ability to neutralize negative energies. This translucent brown to black crystal derives its smoky color from natural irradiation of quartz during its formation. Smoky Quartz is valued for its grounding properties and its ability to dissipate negative energies and emotions.

Properties and Uses of Smoky Quartz

Smoky Quartz is a stone of grounding and protection, providing a strong link to the Earth and the base chakra. It helps to anchor and stabilize while offering protection from negative energies. This crystal also promotes personal pride and joy in living, dispels nightmares, and manifests your dreams.

Cleansing and Charging Smoky Quartz

To cleanse Smoky Quartz, pass it through sage smoke or bury it in the earth overnight. Charging Smoky Quartz can be done by placing it under the light of the full moon or sunlight for several hours. Its grounding energy responds well to natural elements, revitalizing its protective properties.

<u>Smoky Quartz Spells</u>

Grounding and Stability Spell

Purpose: To promote grounding and stability.

Materials: Smoky Quartz, brown candle.

Instructions: Light the brown candle, hold the Smoky Quartz, and visualize roots extending from your body into the earth, grounding you deeply.

Negativity Dissipation Spell

Purpose: To dissipate negative energies.

Materials: Smoky Quartz, black candle.

Instructions: Light the black candle, hold the Smoky Quartz, and visualize it absorbing and transmuting negative energies into positive ones.

Dream Manifestation Spell

Purpose: To manifest your dreams into reality.

Materials: Smoky Quartz, purple candle, dream journal.

Instructions: Light the purple candle, hold the Smoky Quartz, and write down your dreams and aspirations in the dream journal while visualizing them manifesting.

Protection Spell

Purpose: To protect against psychic attacks.

Materials: Smoky Quartz, white candle.

Instructions: Light the white candle, hold the Smoky Quartz, and visualize a protective shield forming around you, deflecting negative energies.

Joy and Positivity Spell

Purpose: To attract joy and positivity.

Materials: Smoky Quartz, yellow candle.

Instructions: Light the yellow candle, hold the Smoky Quartz, and focus on feelings of joy and positivity filling your heart and space.

Anxiety Relief Spell

Purpose: To alleviate anxiety.

Materials: Smoky Quartz, blue candle, calming tea.

Instructions: Light the blue candle, hold the Smoky Quartz, and drink calming tea while visualizing anxiety dissipating.

Energy Cleansing Spell

Purpose: To cleanse your personal energy.

Materials: Smoky Quartz, white candle, sage bundle.

Instructions: Light the white candle, burn sage, and pass the Smoky Quartz through the sage smoke while visualizing it purifying your energy field.

Inner Strength Spell

Purpose: To enhance inner strength.

Materials: Smoky Quartz, red candle.

Instructions: Light the red candle, hold the Smoky Quartz, and visualize its grounding energy strengthening your resolve and inner fortitude.

Balance Spell

Purpose: To achieve balance in life.

Materials: Smoky Quartz, green candle.

Instructions: Light the green candle, hold the Smoky Quartz, and meditate while focusing on achieving balance and harmony in all aspects of your life.

Psychic Protection Spell

Purpose: To protect against psychic interference.

Materials: Smoky Quartz, silver candle.

Instructions: Light the silver candle, hold the Smoky Quartz, and visualize a barrier of light forming around you, shielding you from psychic intrusions.

Release Negativity Spell

Purpose: To release negative emotions and thoughts.

Materials: Smoky Quartz, black candle, fire-safe bowl.

Instructions: Light the black candle, hold the Smoky Quartz, and write down negative emotions or thoughts on paper. Burn the paper in the fire-safe bowl while visualizing them dissipating.

Healing Spell

Purpose: To promote physical and emotional healing.

Materials: Smoky Quartz, green candle, healing herbs.

Instructions: Light the green candle, hold the Smoky Quartz, and visualize healing energy enveloping and restoring your body and spirit.

Manifestation Spell

Purpose: To manifest desires into reality.

Materials: Smoky Quartz, purple candle, manifestation journal.

Instructions: Light the purple candle, hold the Smoky Quartz, and write down your desires in the manifestation journal while visualizing them coming true.

Spiritual Protection Spell

Purpose: To protect against spiritual attacks.

Materials: Smoky Quartz, white candle, incense.

Instructions: Light the white candle, burn incense, and hold the Smoky Quartz while visualizing a protective barrier around your spiritual space.

Self-Discovery Spell

Purpose: To promote self-discovery.

Materials: Smoky Quartz, yellow candle, journal.

Instructions: Light the yellow candle, hold the Smoky Quartz, and journal about your inner thoughts and discoveries.

Clarity and Focus Spell

Purpose: To enhance mental clarity and focus.

Materials: Smoky Quartz, blue candle.

Instructions: Light the blue candle, hold the Smoky Quartz, and clear your mind while focusing on clarity and sharpness of thought.

Prosperity Spell

Purpose: To attract prosperity and abundance.

Materials: Smoky Quartz, green candle, symbols of prosperity.

Instructions: Light the green candle, hold the Smoky Quartz, and visualize opportunities and abundance flowing into your life.

Peaceful Sleep Spell

Purpose: To promote restful sleep and dreams.

Materials: Smoky Quartz, lavender candle.

Instructions: Light the lavender candle, hold the Smoky Quartz, and envision peaceful sleep and dreams throughout the night.

Confidence Spell

Purpose: To boost self-confidence.

Materials: Smoky Quartz, yellow candle, mirror.

Instructions: Light the yellow candle, hold the Smoky Quartz, and look into the mirror while affirming your confidence and self-worth.

Love Spell

Purpose: To attract love and deepen relationships.

Materials: Smoky Quartz, pink candle.

Instructions: Light the pink candle, hold the Smoky Quartz, and visualize love and harmony in your relationships.

Protection During Travel Spell

Purpose: To protect during travel.

Materials: Smoky Quartz, white candle, travel token.

Instructions: Light the white candle, hold the Smoky Quartz, and place the travel token next to it while visualizing safe travels.

Strength and Endurance Spell

Purpose: To enhance strength and endurance.

Materials: Smoky Quartz, red candle.

Instructions: Light the red candle, hold the Smoky Quartz, and visualize yourself filled with strength and endurance to overcome challenges.

Harmony in Relationships Spell

Purpose: To promote harmony in relationships.

Materials: Smoky Quartz, pink candle.

Instructions: Light the pink candle, hold the Smoky Quartz, and visualize loving and harmonious relationships.

Psychic Protection Spell

Purpose: To shield against negative psychic energies.

Materials: Smoky Quartz, black candle.

Instructions: Light the black candle, hold the Smoky Quartz, and visualize a protective barrier forming around your psychic space, shielding you from negative energies and psychic attacks.

Grounding and Centering Spell

Purpose: To promote grounding and inner stability.

Materials: Smoky Quartz, brown candle.

Instructions: Light the brown candle, hold the Smoky Quartz, and imagine roots extending from your body deep into the earth, grounding you firmly to the earth's energy while bringing inner stability and peace.

Smoky Quartz is a stone of grounding and protection, revered for its ability to neutralize negativity and promote stability. By incorporating these spells into your practice, you can harness its energy to ground yourself, protect against negative energies, and manifest your dreams. Embrace the smoky hues and protective qualities of *Smoky Quartz* as you navigate life's challenges with strength and positivity. Each spell deepens your connection to this powerful crystal, guiding you towards a life of grounded stability and emotional resilience.

Garnet

Introduction to Garnet

Garnet is a stone of vitality, passion, and energy, known for its deep red hues. It has been used for centuries as a talisman for protection and strength. Garnet is associated with the root chakra and is believed to enhance creativity, passion, and success in various endeavors.

Properties and Uses of Garnet

Garnet is a stone of regeneration and energizing, providing vitality and strength to its wearer. It stimulates the flow of energy throughout the body and balances the emotional state. This crystal promotes courage, confidence, and perseverance, making it ideal for those pursuing their goals with determination.

Cleansing and Charging Garnet

To cleanse Garnet, rinse it under cool running water or cleanse it with sage smoke. Charging Garnet can be done by placing it on a bed of hematite stones or under the light of the full moon. Its vibrant energy responds well to natural elements, revitalizing its properties.

Garnet Spells

Passion and Creativity Spell

Purpose: To enhance passion and creativity.

Materials: Garnet, red candle.

Instructions: Light the red candle, hold the Garnet, and engage in creative activities while allowing passion to flow freely.

Energy Boost Spell

Purpose: To boost energy levels.

Materials: Garnet, orange candle.

Instructions: Light the orange candle, hold the Garnet, and visualize its energy infusing you with vitality and strength.

Courage and Confidence Spell

Purpose: To boost courage and confidence.

Materials: Garnet, yellow candle.

Instructions: Light the yellow candle, hold the Garnet, and affirm your courage and confidence in achieving your goals.

Physical Vitality Spell

Purpose: To promote physical vitality.

Materials: Garnet, green candle.

Instructions: Light the green candle, hold the Garnet, and visualize it enhancing your physical vitality and well-being.

Success in Endeavors Spell

Purpose: To attract success in endeavors.

Materials: Garnet, gold candle.

Instructions: Light the gold candle, hold the Garnet, and visualize success flowing into your life.

Emotional Stability Spell

Purpose: To achieve emotional stability.

Materials: Garnet, blue candle.

Instructions: Light the blue candle, hold the Garnet, and meditate while focusing on emotional balance and harmony.

Protection from Negativity Spell

Purpose: To shield against negativity.

Materials: Garnet, black candle.

Instructions: Light the black candle, hold the Garnet, and visualize it forming a protective shield around you, deflecting negativity.

Heart Healing Spell

Purpose: To heal emotional wounds of the heart.

Materials: Garnet, pink candle.

Instructions: Light the pink candle, hold the Garnet, and focus on healing and nurturing your heart.

Motivation Spell

Purpose: To boost motivation.

Materials: Garnet, purple candle.

Instructions: Light the purple candle, hold the Garnet, and affirm your motivation to achieve your goals.

Grounding and Stability Spell

Purpose: To promote grounding and stability.

Materials: Garnet, brown candle.

Instructions: Light the brown candle, hold the Garnet, and visualize roots extending from your body into the earth, grounding you deeply.

Prosperity Spell

Purpose: To attract prosperity and abundance.

Materials: Garnet, green candle, coins or symbols of prosperity.

Instructions: Light the green candle, hold the Garnet, and visualize opportunities and abundance flowing into your life.

Passion and Vitality Spell

Purpose: To ignite passion and vitality.

Materials: Garnet, red candle.

Instructions: Light the red candle, hold the Garnet, and feel the surge of passion and vitality coursing through you.

Self-Confidence Spell

Purpose: To boost self-confidence.

Materials: Garnet, yellow candle.

Instructions: Light the yellow candle, hold the Garnet, and affirm your self-confidence and inner strength.

Spiritual Growth Spell

Purpose: To enhance spiritual growth.

Materials: Garnet, purple candle.

Instructions: Light the purple candle, hold the Garnet, and meditate while focusing on spiritual insight and growth.

Energy Cleansing Spell

Purpose: To cleanse negative energy.

Materials: Garnet, white candle.

Instructions: Light the white candle, hold the Garnet, and visualize it purifying your energy field.

Harmony in Relationships Spell

Purpose: To promote harmony in relationships.

Materials: Garnet, pink candle.

Instructions: Light the pink candle, hold the Garnet, and visualize loving and harmonious relationships.

Career Success Spell

Purpose: To achieve success in career endeavors.

Materials: Garnet, green candle.

Instructions: Light the green candle, hold the Garnet, and envision career success and recognition.

Balance and Alignment Spell

Purpose: To achieve balance and alignment.

Materials: Garnet, blue candle.

Instructions: Light the blue candle, hold the Garnet, and focus on balancing your energies and aligning with your true purpose.

Strength and Endurance Spell

Purpose: To enhance strength and endurance.

Materials: Garnet, red candle.

Instructions: Light the red candle, hold the Garnet, and visualize yourself filled with strength and endurance to overcome challenges.

Wisdom and Insight Spell

Purpose: To gain wisdom and insight.

Materials: Garnet, purple candle.

Instructions: Light the purple candle, hold the Garnet, and meditate while seeking wisdom and deeper understanding.

Friendship Spell

Purpose: To attract new friendships or strengthen existing ones.

Materials: Garnet, pink candle.

Instructions: Light the pink candle, hold the Garnet, and visualize yourself surrounded by loyal and supportive friends.

Clarity of Mind Spell

Purpose: To achieve mental clarity and focus.

Materials: Garnet, blue candle.

Instructions: Light the blue candle, hold the Garnet, and clear your mind of distractions, focusing on clarity and sharpness of thought.

Peaceful Sleep Spell

Purpose: To promote restful and peaceful sleep.

Materials: Garnet, white candle.

Instructions: Light the white candle, hold the Garnet, and envision calmness and tranquility enveloping you as you drift into deep sleep.

Protection During Travel Spell

Purpose: To protect during travel.

Materials: Garnet, blue candle.

Instructions: Light the blue candle, hold the Garnet, and visualize a protective shield surrounding you as you embark on your journey.

Garnet is a stone of passion, strength, and vitality, revered for its ability to energize and protect. By incorporating these spells into your practice, you can harness its energy to boost creativity, enhance courage, and attract success. Embrace the deep red hues and vibrant qualities of Garnet as you pursue your passions with determination and vigor. Each spell deepens your connection to this powerful crystal, guiding you towards a life filled with vitality and achievement.

Aquamarine

Introduction to Aquamarine

Aquamarine is a calming and soothing stone with hues ranging from light blue to greenish-blue. Its name is derived from the Latin words for "water of the sea," reflecting its tranquil and oceanic qualities. Aquamarine is associated with the throat chakra and is believed to promote courage, clear communication, and stress relief.

Properties and Uses of Aquamarine

Aquamarine is a stone of courage and protection, often carried by sailors as a talisman for safe travels across the seas. It enhances clarity of thought and aids in clear communication, making it ideal for resolving conflicts and expressing oneself with confidence. This crystal also soothes fears and anxieties, promoting a sense of peace and tranquility.

Cleansing and Charging Aquamarine

To cleanse Aquamarine, rinse it under cool running water or cleanse it with sea salt. Charging Aquamarine can be done by placing it in sunlight or under the light of the full moon. Its calming energy responds well to natural elements, revitalizing its soothing properties.

Aquamarine Spells

Courage and Confidence Spell

Purpose: To boost courage and confidence.

Materials: Aquamarine, yellow candle.

Instructions: Light the yellow candle, hold the Aquamarine, and affirm your courage and confidence in challenging situations.

Stress Relief Spell

Purpose: To alleviate stress and anxiety.

Materials: Aquamarine, blue candle, calming incense.

Instructions: Light the blue candle, hold the Aquamarine, and burn calming incense while visualizing stress melting away.

Communication Spell

Purpose: To enhance clear communication.

Materials: Aquamarine, turquoise candle.

Instructions: Light the turquoise candle, hold the Aquamarine, and focus on speaking clearly and effectively.

Peace and Serenity Spell

Purpose: To promote peace and serenity.

Materials: Aquamarine, white candle.

Instructions: Light the white candle, hold the Aquamarine, and meditate while focusing on inner peace and tranquility.

Protection during Travel Spell

Purpose: To protect during travel.

Materials: Aquamarine, blue candle, travel token.

Instructions: Light the blue candle, hold the Aquamarine, and place a travel token next to it while visualizing safe and smooth travels.

Emotional Healing Spell

Purpose: To heal emotional wounds.

Materials: Aquamarine, pink candle.

Instructions: Light the pink candle, hold the Aquamarine, and focus on healing emotional pain and nurturing your heart.

Clarity of Mind Spell

Purpose: To enhance mental clarity.

Materials: Aquamarine, lavender candle.

Instructions: Light the lavender candle, hold the Aquamarine, and meditate while focusing on clear and focused thoughts.

Courage to Face Challenges Spell

Purpose: To find courage to face challenges.

Materials: Aquamarine, orange candle.

Instructions: Light the orange candle, hold the Aquamarine, and visualize yourself overcoming obstacles with courage and determination.

Patience and Tolerance Spell

Purpose: To cultivate patience and tolerance.

Materials: Aquamarine, light blue candle.

Instructions: Light the light blue candle, hold the Aquamarine, and meditate while focusing on cultivating patience and tolerance in challenging situations.

Healing Waters Spell

Purpose: To draw upon the calming energies of water.

Materials: Aquamarine, bowl of water.

Instructions: Place the Aquamarine in the bowl of water and meditate while visualizing the soothing and healing energies of water washing over you.

Courage to Take Risks Spell

Purpose: To gather courage to take risks.

Materials: Aquamarine, red candle.

Instructions: Light the red candle, hold the Aquamarine, and visualize yourself stepping forward with courage and confidence.

Self-Expression Spell

Purpose: To enhance self-expression.

Materials: Aquamarine, sky blue candle.

Instructions: Light the sky blue candle, hold the Aquamarine, and express yourself freely in words or art.

Manifestation of Dreams Spell

Purpose: To manifest your dreams into reality.

Materials: Aquamarine, purple candle, dream journal.

Instructions: Light the purple candle, hold the Aquamarine, and write down your dreams and aspirations in the dream journal while visualizing them manifesting.

Inspiration Spell

Purpose: To attract inspiration.

Materials: Aquamarine, silver candle.

Instructions: Light the silver candle, hold the Aquamarine, and open yourself to receive creative inspiration.

Harmony in Relationships Spell

Purpose: To promote harmony in relationships.

Materials: Aquamarine, pink candle.

Instructions: Light the pink candle, hold the Aquamarine, and visualize peaceful and loving relationships.

Spiritual Growth Spell

Purpose: To enhance spiritual growth.

Materials: Aquamarine, violet candle.

Instructions: Light the violet candle, hold the Aquamarine, and meditate while focusing on spiritual enlightenment.

Confidence in Public Speaking Spell

Purpose: To boost confidence in public speaking.

Materials: Aquamarine, gold candle.

Instructions: Light the gold candle, hold the Aquamarine, and visualize yourself speaking confidently and eloquently.

Decision-Making Clarity Spell

Purpose: To gain clarity in decision-making.

Materials: Aquamarine, green candle.

Instructions: Light the green candle, hold the Aquamarine, and focus on clarity and wisdom in making decisions.

Protection from Psychic Attacks Spell

Purpose: To shield against psychic attacks.

Materials: Aquamarine, black candle.

Instructions: Light the black candle, hold the Aquamarine, and visualize a protective barrier surrounding you.

Career Success Spell

Purpose: To attract success in career endeavors.

Materials: Aquamarine, brown candle.

Instructions: Light the brown candle, hold the Aquamarine, and visualize career success and recognition.

Friendship Bond Strengthening Spell

Purpose: To strengthen bonds of friendship.

Materials: Aquamarine, light green candle.

Instructions: Light the light green candle, hold the Aquamarine, and visualize your friendships growing stronger and more supportive.

Positive Outlook Spell

Purpose: To cultivate a positive outlook.

Materials: Aquamarine, sunflower yellow candle.

Instructions: Light the sunflower yellow candle, hold the Aquamarine, and focus on seeing the bright side of situations.

Physical Healing Spell

Purpose: To promote physical healing.

Materials: Aquamarine, green candle, healing herbs.

Instructions: Light the green candle, hold the Aquamarine, and visualize healing energy flowing through you.

Financial Abundance Spell

Purpose: To attract financial abundance.

Materials: Aquamarine, green candle, coins or symbols of prosperity.

Instructions: Light the green candle, hold the Aquamarine, and visualize financial abundance and prosperity.

Success in Studies Spell

Purpose: To achieve success in studies.

Materials: Aquamarine, blue candle, study materials.

Instructions: Light the blue candle, hold the Aquamarine, and study while focusing on understanding and retaining information.

Aquamarine is a stone of courage, communication, and tranquility, revered for its calming properties and association with the sea. By incorporating these spells into your practice, you can harness its energy to promote clear communication, alleviate stress, and find inner peace. Embrace the serene blue hues and tranquil qualities of Aquamarine as you navigate life's challenges with courage and grace. Each spell deepens your connection to this soothing crystal, guiding you towards a life filled with clarity and emotional healing.

Moonstone

Introduction to Moonstone

Moonstone is a captivating crystal known for its iridescent beauty and mystical properties. It is associated with the energy of the moon and is revered for its ability to enhance intuition, balance emotions, and promote spiritual growth.

Properties and Uses of Moonstone

Moonstone is a stone of inner growth and strength, offering protection and inspiration. It soothes emotional instability and stress, stabilizes emotions, and provides calmness. This crystal also enhances intuition, promotes inspiration, success, and good fortune in love and business matters.

Cleansing and Charging Moonstone

To keep Moonstone working at its best, cleanse it regularly using methods like running water, moonlight, or smudging with sage. Charging can be done under moonlight or with other crystals like Selenite to amplify its energies.

Moonstone Spells

Intuition Enhancement Spell

Purpose: To enhance intuition and inner wisdom.

Materials: Moonstone, indigo candle.

Instructions: Light the indigo candle, hold the Moonstone, and meditate on opening your intuition to receive guidance.

Emotional Balance Spell

Purpose: To achieve emotional stability and harmony.

Materials: Moonstone, blue candle.

Instructions: Light the blue candle, hold the Moonstone, and visualize emotional balance and peace.

New Beginnings Spell

Purpose: To attract new opportunities and beginnings.

Materials: Moonstone, white candle.

Instructions: Light the white candle, hold the Moonstone, and visualize new opportunities coming into your life.

Divination Spell

Purpose: To enhance divination abilities.

Materials: Moonstone, purple candle.

Instructions: Light the purple candle, hold the Moonstone, and focus on receiving clear insights during divination practices.

Love and Compassion Spell

Purpose: To attract love and foster compassion.

Materials: Moonstone, pink candle.

Instructions: Light the pink candle, hold the Moonstone, and focus on attracting love and fostering compassion in your relationships.

Protection Spell

Purpose: To protect against negative energies.

Materials: Moonstone, black candle.

Instructions: Light the black candle, hold the Moonstone, and visualize a protective shield surrounding you.

Inner Peace Spell

Purpose: To promote inner peace and serenity.

Materials: Moonstone, green candle.

Instructions: Light the green candle, hold the Moonstone, and meditate on feelings of calmness and tranquility.

Prosperity Spell

Purpose: To attract prosperity and abundance.

Materials: Moonstone, green candle, prosperity herbs (such as basil or cinnamon).

Instructions: Light the green candle, hold the Moonstone, and sprinkle prosperity herbs around it while visualizing abundance flowing into your life.

Dream Enhancement Spell

Purpose: To enhance dreams and intuition.

Materials: Moonstone, lavender candle.

Instructions: Light the lavender candle, hold the Moonstone, and place it under your pillow to enhance dreams and intuitive insights.

Healing Spell

Purpose: To promote physical and emotional healing.

Materials: Moonstone, blue candle, healing crystals.

Instructions: Light the blue candle, hold the Moonstone, and surround yourself with healing crystals while visualizing healing energy enveloping you.

Balance Spell

Purpose: To restore balance and harmony.

Materials: Moonstone, white candle.

Instructions: Light the white candle, hold the Moonstone, and visualize a state of balance and harmony in all aspects of your life.

Self-Love Spell

Purpose: To cultivate self-love and acceptance.

Materials: Moonstone, rose quartz, pink candle.

Instructions: Light the pink candle, hold the Moonstone and rose quartz, and affirm self-love and acceptance while feeling their energies enveloping you.

Creativity Spell

Purpose: To enhance creativity and inspiration.

Materials: Moonstone, orange candle, artistic materials.

Instructions: Light the orange candle, hold the Moonstone, and engage in creative activities while allowing inspiration to flow.

Manifestation Spell

Purpose: To manifest desires and goals.

Materials: Moonstone, green candle, manifestation journal.

Instructions: Light the green candle, hold the Moonstone, and write down your desires in the manifestation journal while visualizing them manifesting into reality.

Strength Spell

Purpose: To boost inner strength and resilience.

Materials: Moonstone, red candle.

Instructions: Light the red candle, hold the Moonstone, and affirm your inner strength and resilience in facing challenges.

Psychic Protection Spell

Purpose: To shield against negative psychic energies.

Materials: Moonstone, amethyst, purple candle.

Instructions: Light the purple candle, hold the Moonstone and amethyst, and visualize a protective shield around your aura.

Joy and Happiness Spell

Purpose: To attract joy and happiness into your life.

Materials: Moonstone, yellow candle.

Instructions: Light the yellow candle, hold the Moonstone, and focus on feelings of joy and happiness filling your heart.

Spiritual Connection Spell

Purpose: To deepen spiritual connections.

Materials: Moonstone, white candle, sacred space.

Instructions: Light the white candle, hold the Moonstone, and meditate in your sacred space to deepen spiritual connections.

Focus and Concentration Spell

Purpose: To improve focus and mental clarity.

Materials: Moonstone, white candle.

Instructions: Light the white candle, hold the Moonstone, and visualize clear focus and mental clarity.

Gratitude Spell

Purpose: To cultivate gratitude and appreciation.

Materials: Moonstone, yellow candle.

Instructions: Light the yellow candle, hold the Moonstone, and reflect on things you are grateful for while feeling gratitude filling your heart.

Relationship Harmony Spell

Purpose: To promote harmony and understanding in relationships.

Materials: Moonstone, pink candle, photo of loved ones.

Instructions: Light the pink candle, hold the Moonstone, and visualize harmony and understanding in your relationships.

Wisdom Spell

Purpose: To attract wisdom and insight.

Materials: Moonstone, blue candle.

Instructions: Light the blue candle, hold the Moonstone, and meditate on receiving wisdom and insight into important matters.

Empowerment Spell

Purpose: To feel empowered and confident.

Materials: Moonstone, gold candle, mirror.

Instructions: Light the gold candle, hold the Moonstone, and look into the mirror while affirming your empowerment and capabilities.

Peaceful Sleep Spell

Purpose: To promote peaceful sleep and relaxation.

Materials: Moonstone, lavender candle.

Instructions: Light the lavender candle, hold the Moonstone, and place it under your pillow to promote restful sleep and relaxation.

Astral Projection Spell

Purpose: To facilitate astral projection and spiritual journeys.

Materials: Moonstone, silver candle.

Instructions: Light the silver candle, hold the Moonstone, and meditate while focusing on astral projection or spiritual journeys.

Moonstone is a crystal of intuition, inner growth, and divine feminine energy. By integrating these spells into your spiritual practice, you can harness its mystical energy to enhance intuition, foster emotional balance, and connect with the cycles of the moon. Embrace the ethereal beauty of Moonstone as you navigate your spiritual journey and deepen your connection to inner wisdom. Each spell enriches your bond with this enchanting crystal, guiding you towards profound insights and spiritual awakening.

Ruby

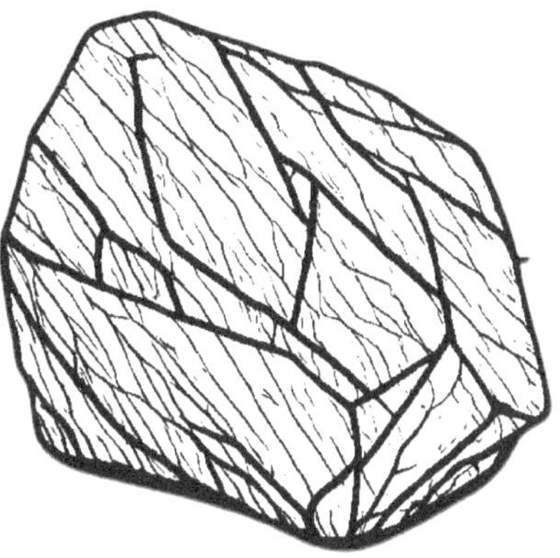

Introduction to Ruby

Ruby is a vibrant red crystal known for its passionate energy and association with vitality, courage, and love. It has been cherished throughout history for its deep color and powerful metaphysical properties. Ruby inspires passion, enhances motivation, and stimulates the heart chakra, fostering love and emotional well-being.

Properties and Uses of Ruby

Ruby is a stone of vitality and strength, activating the root and heart chakras to bring balance and passion into one's life. It encourages confidence, courage, and assertiveness, making it an ideal companion for those seeking to pursue their dreams with determination. Ruby also enhances creativity, stimulates the mind, and attracts prosperity and abundance.

Cleansing and Charging Ruby

To keep Ruby working at its best, cleanse it by placing it under cool running water or smudging it with sage. Charging Ruby can be done under the light of the sun or with other crystals like Carnelian to amplify its energies.

Ruby Spells

Passion and Vitality Spell

Purpose: To ignite passion and enhance vitality.

Materials: Ruby, red candle.

Instructions: Light the red candle, hold the Ruby, and visualize vibrant energy filling your body with passion and vitality.

Courage and Confidence Spell

Purpose: To boost courage and self-confidence.

Materials: Ruby, yellow candle.

Instructions: Light the yellow candle, hold the Ruby, and affirm your courage and confidence in achieving your goals.

Love and Emotional Healing Spell

Purpose: To promote love and heal emotional wounds.

Materials: Ruby, pink candle.

Instructions: Light the pink candle, hold the Ruby, and focus on sending love to heal emotional pain and foster emotional well-being.

Creativity and Inspiration Spell

Purpose: To enhance creativity and attract inspiration.

Materials: Ruby, orange candle, artistic materials.

Instructions: Light the orange candle, hold the Ruby, and engage in creative activities while allowing inspiration to flow freely.

Prosperity and Abundance Spell

Purpose: To attract prosperity and abundance into your life.

Materials: Ruby, green candle, prosperity herbs (such as basil or cinnamon).

Instructions: Light the green candle, hold the Ruby, and sprinkle prosperity herbs around it while visualizing a steady flow of prosperity and abundance.

Strength and Endurance Spell

Purpose: To enhance physical strength and endurance.

Materials: Ruby, red candle, exercise equipment.

Instructions: Light the red candle, hold the Ruby, and engage in physical exercise while feeling strong and enduring.

Passionate Relationships Spell

Purpose: To foster passionate and loving relationships.

Materials: Ruby, pink candle, photo of loved ones.

Instructions: Light the pink candle, hold the Ruby, and visualize harmony and passion in your relationships.

Courage in Love Spell

Purpose: To find courage in matters of the heart.

Materials: Ruby, pink candle, rose quartz.

Instructions: Light the pink candle, hold the Ruby and rose quartz, and affirm your courage to pursue love and emotional fulfillment.

Fire Energy Spell

Purpose: To harness the fiery energy of Ruby.

Materials: Ruby, red candle.

Instructions: Light the red candle, hold the Ruby, and meditate while feeling the intense energy and power of Ruby flowing through you.

Joy and Happiness Spell

Purpose: To attract joy and happiness into your life.

Materials: Ruby, yellow candle.

Instructions: Light the yellow candle, hold the Ruby, and focus on feelings of joy and happiness filling your heart.

Protection and Strength Spell

Purpose: To protect against negative energies and enhance inner strength.

Materials: Ruby, black candle.

Instructions: Light the black candle, hold the Ruby, and visualize a protective shield of Ruby's energy surrounding you.

Self-Confidence Spell

Purpose: To boost self-confidence and assertiveness.

Materials: Ruby, yellow candle.

Instructions: Light the yellow candle, hold the Ruby, and affirm your self-worth and confidence in all situations.

Emotional Balance Spell

Purpose: To achieve emotional balance and harmony.

Materials: Ruby, pink candle.

Instructions: Light the pink candle, hold the Ruby, and visualize emotional equilibrium and peace filling your being.

Manifestation of Desires Spell

Purpose: To manifest your desires into reality.

Materials: Ruby, green candle, written goals.

Instructions: Light the green candle, hold the Ruby, and focus on your desires manifesting with Ruby's energetic support.

Heart Healing Spell

Purpose: To heal and strengthen the heart chakra.

Materials: Ruby, green candle, rose quartz.

Instructions: Light the green candle, hold the Ruby and rose quartz, and visualize healing energy flowing into your heart chakra.

Success in Career Spell

Purpose: To attract success and advancement in your career.

Materials: Ruby, green candle, business-related items.

Instructions: Light the green candle, hold the Ruby, and visualize career success and prosperity.

Spiritual Growth Spell

Purpose: To stimulate spiritual growth and enlightenment.

Materials: Ruby, white candle.

Instructions: Light the white candle, hold the Ruby, and meditate while focusing on spiritual insights and growth.

Inner Fire Spell

Purpose: To ignite and nurture your inner fire.

Materials: Ruby, red candle.

Instructions: Light the red candle, hold the Ruby, and feel your inner passion and motivation burning brightly.

Protection in Relationships Spell

Purpose: To protect relationships from negativity.

Materials: Ruby, pink candle, photo of loved ones.

Instructions: Light the pink candle, hold the Ruby, and visualize a shield of Ruby's protective energy around your relationships.

Energy Boost Spell

Purpose: To increase overall energy levels.

Materials: Ruby, red candle.

Instructions: Light the red candle, hold the Ruby, and feel revitalizing energy filling your body and mind.

Confidence in Creativity Spell

Purpose: To boost confidence in creative endeavors.

Materials: Ruby, orange candle, artistic materials.

Instructions: Light the orange candle, hold the Ruby, and engage in creative activities while feeling confident and inspired.

Harmony in Family Spell

Purpose: To foster harmony and love within the family.

Materials: Ruby, pink candle, family photo.

Instructions: Light the pink candle, hold the Ruby, and visualize love and harmony flourishing within your family.

Passion in Life Spell

Purpose: To ignite passion and zest for life.

Materials: Ruby, red candle.

Instructions: Light the red candle, hold the Ruby, and affirm your passion and enthusiasm for life's adventures.

Spiritual Protection Spell

Purpose: To shield spiritually against negative influences.

Materials: Ruby, white candle, sacred space.

Instructions: Light the white candle, hold the Ruby, and meditate in your sacred space while feeling spiritually protected.

Ruby is a crystal of passion, vitality, and courage, revered for its ability to ignite the fire within and attract prosperity and love. By incorporating these spells into your practice, you can harness Ruby's energy to enhance creativity, boost confidence, and manifest your desires. Embrace the vibrant energy of Ruby as you journey through life with passion and determination. Each spell deepens your connection to this powerful crystal, empowering you to live passionately and achieve your goals with unwavering courage.

Obsidian

Introduction to Obsidian

Obsidian is a powerful volcanic glass that forms when molten lava cools quickly. It has been used for centuries for its protective and grounding properties. Obsidian is often black but can also appear in other colors such as brown, blue, green, or rainbow sheens. This crystal is associated with transformation, purification, and psychic protection.

Properties and Uses of Obsidian

Obsidian is known for its ability to shield against negativity and absorb negative energies from the environment. It helps to uncover truths, promote introspection, and dispel illusions. Obsidian is a stone of deep soul cleansing, offering powerful protection and grounding for those who work with its energies.

Cleansing and Charging Obsidian

To keep Obsidian working at its best, cleanse it by placing it under running water, burying it in earth or salt, or smudging it with sage. Charging Obsidian can be done under moonlight or with other crystals like Clear Quartz to amplify its protective energies.

Obsidian Spells

Protection Spell

Purpose: To shield against negative energies.

Materials: Obsidian, black candle.

Instructions: Light the black candle, hold the Obsidian, and visualize it forming a protective shield around you.

Grounding Spell

Purpose: To ground yourself in times of stress.

Materials: Obsidian, brown candle, earth element (such as soil or rock).

Instructions: Light the brown candle, hold the Obsidian, and connect with the earth element to stabilize your energy.

Psychic Protection Spell

Purpose: To protect against psychic attacks.

Materials: Obsidian, purple candle.

Instructions: Light the purple candle, hold the Obsidian, and visualize a shield of protective light surrounding your aura.

Truth Seeking Spell

Purpose: To uncover hidden truths.

Materials: Obsidian, blue candle.

Instructions: Light the blue candle, hold the Obsidian, and meditate on gaining clarity and insight into a specific situation.

Spiritual Cleansing Spell

Purpose: To cleanse your spiritual space.

Materials: Obsidian, white candle, sage.

Instructions: Light the white candle, hold the Obsidian, and burn sage while visualizing your space being cleansed of negative energies.

Emotional Healing Spell

Purpose: To heal emotional wounds.

Materials: Obsidian, pink candle, calming crystals.

Instructions: Light the pink candle, hold the Obsidian, and place calming crystals around you while visualizing emotional wounds healing.

Self-Reflection Spell

Purpose: To promote self-reflection and introspection.

Materials: Obsidian, mirror.

Instructions: Look into the mirror while holding the Obsidian and reflect on your thoughts, feelings, and desires for personal growth.

Balance and Harmony Spell

Purpose: To restore balance and harmony.

Materials: Obsidian, green candle.

Instructions: Light the green candle, hold the Obsidian, and visualize a state of inner balance and harmony.

Protection during Travel Spell

Purpose: To protect during journeys.

Materials: Obsidian, white candle, travel token.

Instructions: Light the white candle, hold the Obsidian, and place the travel token near it while visualizing safe travels.

Release Negativity Spell

Purpose: To release negative attachments.

Materials: Obsidian, black candle.

Instructions: Light the black candle, hold the Obsidian, and visualize negative energies dissolving and leaving your aura.

Courage and Strength Spell

Purpose: To boost courage and inner strength.

Materials: Obsidian, red candle.

Instructions: Light the red candle, hold the Obsidian, and affirm your courage and strength in overcoming challenges.

Psychic Awareness Spell

Purpose: To enhance psychic abilities.

Materials: Obsidian, indigo candle.

Instructions: Light the indigo candle, hold the Obsidian, and meditate on opening your psychic senses.

Prosperity Spell

Purpose: To attract prosperity.

Materials: Obsidian, green candle, prosperity herbs (such as basil or cinnamon).

Instructions: Light the green candle, hold the Obsidian, and sprinkle prosperity herbs around it while visualizing a flow of prosperity into your life.

Dream Protection Spell

Purpose: To protect dreams from negative influences.

Materials: Obsidian, blue candle.

Instructions: Light the blue candle, hold the Obsidian, and place it near your bed to safeguard your dreams.

Clarity and Focus Spell

Purpose: To enhance mental clarity and focus.

Materials: Obsidian, white candle.

Instructions: Light the white candle, hold the Obsidian, and visualize clear thoughts and focused energy.

Personal Empowerment Spell

Purpose: To feel empowered and capable.

Materials: Obsidian, gold candle, mirror.

Instructions: Light the gold candle, hold the Obsidian, and look into the mirror while affirming your empowerment.

Spiritual Protection Spell

Purpose: To protect spiritually against negative influences.

Materials: Obsidian, white candle, sacred space.

Instructions: Light the white candle, hold the Obsidian, and meditate in your sacred space while feeling spiritually protected.

Aura Strengthening Spell

Purpose: To strengthen your aura.

Materials: Obsidian, purple candle.

Instructions: Light the purple candle, hold the Obsidian, and visualize your aura becoming stronger and more resilient.

Relationship Harmony Spell

Purpose: To promote harmony in relationships.

Materials: Obsidian, pink candle, photo of loved ones.

Instructions: Light the pink candle, hold the Obsidian, and visualize harmony and understanding in your relationships.

Wisdom and Insight Spell

Purpose: To gain wisdom and insight.

Materials: Obsidian, yellow candle.

Instructions: Light the yellow candle, hold the Obsidian, and meditate on receiving guidance and understanding.

Protection from Psychic Vampires Spell

Purpose: To shield against energy vampires.

Materials: Obsidian, black candle.

Instructions: Light the black candle, hold the Obsidian, and visualize a shield protecting your energy from draining influences.

Physical Healing Spell

Purpose: To promote physical healing.

Materials: Obsidian, blue candle, healing crystals.

Instructions: Light the blue candle, hold the Obsidian, and place healing crystals around you while visualizing health and vitality.

Manifestation of Goals Spell

Purpose: To manifest your goals and desires.

Materials: Obsidian, green candle, list of goals.

Instructions: Light the green candle, hold the Obsidian, and focus on your goals while visualizing them coming to fruition.

Energy Protection Spell

Purpose: To shield against negative energies.

Materials: Obsidian, black candle.

Instructions: Light the black candle, hold the Obsidian, and visualize it forming a protective shield around you.

Obsidian is a powerful stone of protection and transformation. By incorporating these spells into your practice, you can harness its energy to shield against negativity, cleanse spiritual energies, and promote personal growth. Embrace the deep cleansing power of Obsidian as you navigate through shadow work and emotional healing. Each spell deepens your connection to this volcanic glass, offering you strength, protection, and clarity on your spiritual journey.

Emerald

Introduction to Emerald

Emerald is a lustrous green gemstone known for its beauty and healing properties. It has been revered throughout history for its association with love, prosperity, and growth. This precious stone ranges in color from vivid green to deep Emerald, symbolizing renewal and vitality. Emerald is often called the "Stone of Successful Love," bringing harmony and balance to relationships while enhancing intuition and spiritual awareness.

Properties and Uses of Emerald

Emerald is a stone of heart-centered wisdom and compassion, promoting loyalty, friendship, and unity. It stimulates the heart chakra, encouraging love, abundance, and emotional healing. This crystal is also known for its ability to attract prosperity and enhance creativity, making it a valuable ally for manifesting goals and dreams.

Cleansing and Charging Emerald

To keep Emerald vibrant and effective, cleanse it regularly using methods like running water, sunlight, or moonlight. Charging Emerald can be done by placing it on a bed of quartz crystals or visualizing it being bathed in pure, loving energy.

Emerald Spells

Love and Harmony Spell

Purpose: To attract love and harmony into relationships.

Materials: Emerald, pink candle.

Instructions: Light the pink candle, hold the Emerald, and visualize love and harmony filling your relationships.

Prosperity and Abundance Spell

Purpose: To attract prosperity and abundance.

Materials: Emerald, green candle, prosperity herbs (such as basil or cinnamon).

Instructions: Light the green candle, hold the Emerald, and sprinkle prosperity herbs around it while visualizing a flow of abundance into your life.

Heart Healing Spell

Purpose: To heal emotional wounds and promote heart healing.

Materials: Emerald, pink candle, rose quartz.

Instructions: Light the pink candle, hold the Emerald, and place rose quartz crystals around you while visualizing emotional wounds healing and your heart becoming whole.

Inner Wisdom Spell

Purpose: To connect with inner wisdom and intuition.

Materials: Emerald, indigo candle.

Instructions: Light the indigo candle, hold the Emerald, and meditate on opening your intuition to receive guidance and wisdom.

Communication Enhancement Spell

Purpose: To enhance communication skills.

Materials: Emerald, blue candle.

Instructions: Light the blue candle, hold the Emerald, and visualize clear and effective communication in your personal and professional interactions.

Relationship Renewal Spell

Purpose: To renew and strengthen relationships.

Materials: Emerald, pink candle, photo of loved ones.

Instructions: Light the pink candle, hold the Emerald, and visualize harmony and understanding returning to your relationships.

Health and Vitality Spell

Purpose: To promote health and vitality.

Materials: Emerald, green candle, healing crystals.

Instructions: Light the green candle, hold the Emerald, and place healing crystals around you while visualizing vibrant health and energy.

Confidence and Self-Esteem Spell

Purpose: To boost confidence and self-esteem.

Materials: Emerald, yellow candle.

Instructions: Light the yellow candle, hold the Emerald, and affirm your self-worth and confidence in all aspects of your life.

Creativity Flow Spell

Purpose: To enhance creative inspiration.

Materials: Emerald, green candle, artistic tools.

Instructions: Light the green candle, hold the Emerald, and engage in creative activities while allowing inspiration to flow.

Prosperity Manifestation Spell

Purpose: To manifest prosperity and success.

Materials: Emerald, green candle, list of goals.

Instructions: Light the green candle, hold the Emerald, and focus on your goals while visualizing them manifesting into reality.

Emotional Balance Spell

Purpose: To achieve emotional balance and harmony.

Materials: Emerald, blue candle, calming crystals.

Instructions: Light the blue candle, hold the Emerald, and place calming crystals around you while visualizing emotional balance and tranquility.

Protection from Negative Energy Spell

Purpose: To shield against negative energies.

Materials: Emerald, black candle.

Instructions: Light the black candle, hold the Emerald, and visualize it forming a protective shield around you.

Self-Love Spell

Purpose: To cultivate self-love and acceptance.

Materials: Emerald, pink candle.

Instructions: Light the pink candle, hold the Emerald, and affirm your love and acceptance for yourself.

Decision Making Spell

Purpose: To aid in making clear decisions.

Materials: Emerald, purple candle, list of options.

Instructions: Light the purple candle, hold the Emerald, and focus on gaining clarity and insight into your decisions.

Spiritual Awakening Spell

Purpose: To stimulate spiritual growth and awareness.

Materials: Emerald, white candle.

Instructions: Light the white candle, hold the Emerald, and meditate while focusing on spiritual insights and growth.

Peace and Serenity Spell

Purpose: To promote peace and serenity.

Materials: Emerald, blue candle, calming music.

Instructions: Light the blue candle, hold the Emerald, and listen to calming music while visualizing peace and serenity surrounding you.

Success in Studies or Work Spell

Purpose: To achieve success in studies or work.

Materials: Emerald, yellow candle, study/work materials.

Instructions: Light the yellow candle, hold the Emerald, and visualize success and achievement in your studies or work endeavors.

Dream Enhancement Spell

Purpose: To enhance dreams and intuition.

Materials: Emerald, purple candle.

Instructions: Light the purple candle, hold the Emerald, and place it near your bed to enhance dreams and intuition.

Luck and Fortune Spell

Purpose: To attract luck and fortune.

Materials: Emerald, green candle.

Instructions: Light the green candle, hold the Emerald, and visualize opportunities for luck and fortune coming your way.

Wisdom and Knowledge Spell

Purpose: To attract wisdom and knowledge.

Materials: Emerald, blue candle.

Instructions: Light the blue candle, hold the Emerald, and meditate on receiving wisdom and knowledge.

Gratitude and Blessings Spell

Purpose: To express gratitude and attract blessings.

Materials: Emerald, yellow candle.

Instructions: Light the yellow candle, hold the Emerald, and focus on feelings of gratitude and blessings in your life.

Joy and Happiness Spell

Purpose: To attract joy and happiness.

Materials: Emerald, pink candle.

Instructions: Light the pink candle, hold the Emerald, and visualize feelings of joy and happiness filling your heart.

Spiritual Protection Spell

Purpose: To protect spiritually against negative influences.

Materials: Emerald, white candle, sacred space.

Instructions: Light the white candle, hold the Emerald, and meditate in your sacred space while feeling spiritually protected.

Emerald is a stone of love, prosperity, and growth, revered for its healing energies and ability to enhance intuition. By incorporating these spells into your practice, you can harness its energy to attract love, prosperity, and emotional healing into your life. Embrace the vibrant energy of Emerald as you manifest your goals and nurture your relationships. Each spell deepens your connection to this precious crystal, guiding you on a path of spiritual growth and personal fulfillment.

Peridot

Introduction to Peridot

Peridot is a radiant olive-green gemstone known for its healing properties and connection to nature. Formed deep within the Earth's mantle and brought to the surface by volcanic activity, this crystal is associated with renewal, growth, and abundance. Peridot's bright green hue symbolizes freshness and vitality, making it a powerful stone for healing, prosperity, and spiritual growth.

Properties and Uses of Peridot

Peridot is a crystal of transformation and positive energy, known for its ability to bring healing and protection. It cleanses and purifies the heart chakra, promoting emotional well-being, forgiveness, and compassion. This gemstone also attracts wealth and abundance, enhancing confidence and personal growth. Peridot is often called the "gem of the sun" for its warm, inviting glow that radiates joy and positivity.

Cleansing and Charging Peridot

To maintain Peridot's energetic purity and effectiveness, cleanse it regularly using methods like running water, sunlight, or moonlight. Charging Peridot can be done by placing it on a bed of quartz crystals or in a bowl of sea salt overnight.

Peridot Spells

Heart Healing Spell

Purpose: To heal emotional wounds and promote heart healing.

Materials: Peridot, pink candle, rose quartz.

Instructions: Light the pink candle, hold the Peridot, and place rose quartz crystals around you while visualizing emotional wounds healing and your heart becoming whole.

Self-Love and Acceptance Spell

Purpose: To cultivate self-love and acceptance.

Materials: Peridot, pink candle.

Instructions: Light the pink candle, hold the Peridot, and affirm your love and acceptance for yourself.

Protection from Negative Energies Spell

Purpose: To shield against negative energies.

Materials: Peridot, black candle.

Instructions: Light the black candle, hold the Peridot, and visualize it forming a protective shield around you, repelling negativity.

Joy and Happiness Spell

Purpose: To attract joy and happiness.

Materials: Peridot, yellow candle.

Instructions: Light the yellow candle, hold the Peridot, and visualize feelings of joy and happiness filling your heart and soul.

Abundance and Prosperity Spell

Purpose: To attract abundance and prosperity.

Materials: Peridot, green candle, prosperity herbs (such as basil or cinnamon).

Instructions: Light the green candle, hold the Peridot, and sprinkle prosperity herbs around it while visualizing a flow of abundance into your life.

Renewal and Growth Spell

Purpose: To promote renewal and personal growth.

Materials: Peridot, green candle.

Instructions: Light the green candle, hold the Peridot, and visualize new opportunities for growth and transformation unfolding in your life.

Healing Energy Spell

Purpose: To channel healing energy.

Materials: Peridot, white candle, healing crystals.

Instructions: Light the white candle, hold the Peridot, and place healing crystals around you while visualizing healing energy flowing through your body and spirit.

Confidence Boost Spell

Purpose: To boost confidence and self-assurance.

Materials: Peridot, orange candle.

Instructions: Light the orange candle, hold the Peridot, and affirm your inner strength and confidence.

Communication Enhancement Spell

Purpose: To enhance communication skills.

Materials: Peridot, blue candle.

Instructions: Light the blue candle, hold the Peridot, and visualize clear and effective communication in your personal and professional interactions.

Harmony in Relationships Spell

Purpose: To promote harmony and understanding in relationships.

Materials: Peridot, pink candle, photo of loved ones.

Instructions: Light the pink candle, hold the Peridot, and visualize harmony and love filling your relationships.

Creativity Flow Spell

Purpose: To enhance creative inspiration.

Materials: Peridot, green candle, artistic tools.

Instructions: Light the green candle, hold the Peridot, and engage in creative activities while allowing inspiration to flow freely.

Prosperity Manifestation Spell

Purpose: To manifest prosperity and success.

Materials: Peridot, green candle, list of goals.

Instructions: Light the green candle, hold the Peridot, and focus on your goals while visualizing them manifesting into reality.

Emotional Balance Spell

Purpose: To achieve emotional balance and inner peace.

Materials: Peridot, blue candle, calming crystals.

Instructions: Light the blue candle, hold the Peridot, and place calming crystals around you while visualizing emotional balance and tranquility.

Spiritual Growth Spell

Purpose: To stimulate spiritual growth and awareness.

Materials: Peridot, white candle.

Instructions: Light the white candle, hold the Peridot, and meditate while focusing on spiritual insights and growth.

Decision Making Spell

Purpose: To aid in making clear decisions.

Materials: Peridot, purple candle, list of options.

Instructions: Light the purple candle, hold the Peridot, and focus on gaining clarity and insight into your decisions.

Peace and Serenity Spell

Purpose: To promote peace and serenity.

Materials: Peridot, blue candle, calming music.

Instructions: Light the blue candle, hold the Peridot, and listen to calming music while visualizing peace and serenity surrounding you.

Success in Endeavors Spell

Purpose: To achieve success in endeavors.

Materials: Peridot, gold candle.

Instructions: Light the gold candle, hold the Peridot, and visualize success and achievement in your endeavors.

Energy Clearing Spell

Purpose: To clear and cleanse energy.

Materials: Peridot, white candle, sage.

Instructions: Light the white candle, hold the Peridot, and burn sage while visualizing negative energies being cleared from your aura and environment.

Luck Enhancement Spell

Purpose: To enhance overall luck and good fortune.

Materials: Peridot, green candle, lucky charm.

Instructions: Light the green candle, hold the Peridot, and place the lucky charm near it while visualizing luck flowing into your life.

Vitality and Strength Spell

Purpose: To enhance physical vitality and strength.

Materials: Peridot, red candle, exercise equipment.

Instructions: Light the red candle, hold the Peridot, and engage in physical exercise while feeling strong and energized.

Dream Enhancement Spell

Purpose: To enhance dreams and intuition.

Materials: Peridot, purple candle.

Instructions: Light the purple candle, hold the Peridot, and place it near your bed to enhance dreams and intuition during sleep.

Wisdom and Insight Spell

Purpose: To attract wisdom and insight.

Materials: Peridot, blue candle.

Instructions: Light the blue candle, hold the Peridot, and meditate on receiving wisdom and insight into your life's path.

Gratitude and Blessings Spell

Purpose: To express gratitude and attract blessings.

Materials: Peridot, yellow candle.

Instructions: Light the yellow candle, hold the Peridot, and focus on feelings of gratitude and blessings in your life.

Peridot is a gemstone of healing, prosperity, and spiritual growth, cherished for its radiant energy and connection to nature. By incorporating these spells into your practice, you can harness Peridot's energy to attract abundance, promote emotional healing, and enhance spiritual awareness. Embrace the transformative power of Peridot as you cultivate joy, prosperity, and inner peace in your life. Each spell deepens your connection to this luminous crystal, guiding you on a path of personal growth and fulfillment.

Amazonite

Introduction to Amazonite

Amazonite is a soothing blue-green crystal known for its calming and balancing properties. It is often associated with harmony, communication, and emotional healing. This stone's tranquil energy promotes inner peace and clarity, making it ideal for reducing stress and enhancing creativity.

Properties and Uses of Amazonite

Amazonite is a crystal of truth and courage, encouraging honest communication and self-discovery. It alleviates anxiety and fear, allowing for a deeper understanding of one's emotions and desires. Amazonite also supports manifestation and prosperity, attracting luck and success into the lives of those who work with it.

Cleansing and Charging Amazonite

To maintain Amazonite's energy purity and effectiveness, cleanse it regularly using methods like running water, moonlight, or sage smudging. Charging Amazonite can be done by placing it on a windowsill under the light of the full moon or with clear quartz crystals.

Amazonite Spells

Harmony in Relationships Spell

Purpose: To promote harmony and understanding in relationships.

Materials: Amazonite, pink candle, photo of loved ones.

Instructions: Light the pink candle, hold the Amazonite, and visualize harmony and understanding flowing into your relationships.

Communication Clarity Spell

Purpose: To enhance communication clarity.

Materials: Amazonite, blue candle.

Instructions: Light the blue candle, hold the Amazonite, and focus on clear and effective communication in your interactions.

Manifestation of Goals Spell

Purpose: To manifest your goals and desires.

Materials: Amazonite, green candle, list of goals.

Instructions: Light the green candle, hold the Amazonite, and focus on your goals while visualizing them manifesting into reality.

Confidence Enhancement Spell

Purpose: To boost self-confidence and inner strength.

Materials: Amazonite, yellow candle.

Instructions: Light the yellow candle, hold the Amazonite, and affirm your confidence and inner strength.

Emotional Healing Spell

Purpose: To heal emotional wounds and promote emotional balance.

Materials: Amazonite, pink candle, healing crystals.

Instructions: Light the pink candle, hold the Amazonite, and place healing crystals around you while visualizing emotional wounds healing and emotional balance being restored.

Creativity Boost Spell

Purpose: To enhance creative inspiration.

Materials: Amazonite, green candle, artistic tools.

Instructions: Light the green candle, hold the Amazonite, and engage in creative activities while allowing inspiration to flow freely.

Stress Relief Spell

Purpose: To alleviate stress and promote relaxation.

Materials: Amazonite, white candle.

Instructions: Light the white candle, hold the Amazonite, and visualize stress melting away, leaving you feeling calm and relaxed.

Luck and Prosperity Spell

Purpose: To attract luck and prosperity.

Materials: Amazonite, green candle, prosperity herbs (such as basil or cinnamon).

Instructions: Light the green candle, hold the Amazonite, and sprinkle prosperity herbs around it while visualizing a flow of abundance and prosperity into your life.

Decision Making Spell

Purpose: To aid in making clear decisions.

Materials: Amazonite, purple candle, list of options.

Instructions: Light the purple candle, hold the Amazonite, and focus on gaining clarity and insight into your decisions.

Heart Chakra Healing Spell

Purpose: To balance and heal the heart chakra.

Materials: Amazonite, pink candle, rose quartz.

Instructions: Light the pink candle, hold the Amazonite, and place rose quartz crystals around you while visualizing your heart chakra being cleansed and balanced.

Protection from Negative Energies Spell

Purpose: To shield against negative energies.

Materials: Amazonite, black candle.

Instructions: Light the black candle, hold the Amazonite, and visualize it creating a protective shield around you, repelling negativity.

Joy and Happiness Spell

Purpose: To attract joy and happiness into your life.

Materials: Amazonite, yellow candle.

Instructions: Light the yellow candle, hold the Amazonite, and focus on feelings of joy and happiness filling your heart.

Energy Cleansing Spell

Purpose: To cleanse and purify your energy field.

Materials: Amazonite, white candle, sage.

Instructions: Light the white candle, hold the Amazonite, and burn sage while visualizing your energy field being cleansed and purified.

Strength and Endurance Spell

Purpose: To enhance physical strength and endurance.

Materials: Amazonite, red candle, exercise equipment.

Instructions: Light the red candle, hold the Amazonite, and engage in physical exercise while feeling strong and enduring.

Spiritual Growth Spell

Purpose: To stimulate spiritual growth and insight.

Materials: Amazonite, purple candle.

Instructions: Light the purple candle, hold the Amazonite, and meditate while focusing on spiritual insights and growth.

Positivity and Optimism Spell

Purpose: To foster positivity and optimism.

Materials: Amazonite, yellow candle.

Instructions: Light the yellow candle, hold the Amazonite, and visualize positivity and optimism surrounding you.

Dream Enhancement Spell

Purpose: To enhance dreams and intuition.

Materials: Amazonite, blue candle.

Instructions: Light the blue candle, hold the Amazonite, and place it near your bed to enhance dreams and intuition during sleep.

Self-Discovery Spell

Purpose: To promote self-discovery and personal growth.

Materials: Amazonite, purple candle, journal.

Instructions: Light the purple candle, hold the Amazonite, and journal about your thoughts and insights into self-discovery.

Love and Friendship Spell

Purpose: To attract love and strengthen friendships.

Materials: Amazonite, pink candle, heart-shaped item.

Instructions: Light the pink candle, hold the Amazonite, and visualize love and friendship blossoming in your life.

Protection during Travel Spell

Purpose: To protect during journeys.

Materials: Amazonite, white candle, travel token.

Instructions: Light the white candle, hold the Amazonite, and place the travel token near it while visualizing safe and protected travels.

Harmony in the Home Spell

Purpose: To promote harmony and peace in the home.

Materials: Amazonite, white candle.

Instructions: Light the white candle, hold the Amazonite, and visualize harmony and peace filling your home.

Success in Career Spell

Purpose: To attract success and recognition in career endeavors.

Materials: Amazonite, green candle, business-related item.

Instructions: Light the green candle, hold the Amazonite, and visualize success and recognition in your career.

Patience and Tolerance Spell

Purpose: To cultivate patience and tolerance.

Materials: Amazonite, blue candle.

Instructions: Light the blue candle, hold the Amazonite, and affirm patience and tolerance in your interactions.

Balance and Harmony Spell

Purpose: To achieve balance and harmony in life.

Materials: Amazonite, green candle.

Instructions: Light the green candle, hold the Amazonite, and visualize balance and harmony in all aspects of your life.

Amazonite is a crystal of harmony, communication, and emotional healing, celebrated for its tranquil energy and connection to the heart. By incorporating these spells into your practice, you can harness Amazonite's energy to promote harmony in relationships, enhance creativity, and attract abundance. Embrace the soothing power of Amazonite as you cultivate inner peace, clarity, and positive communication in your life. Each spell deepens your connection to this serene crystal, guiding you on a path of emotional healing and personal growth.

Opal

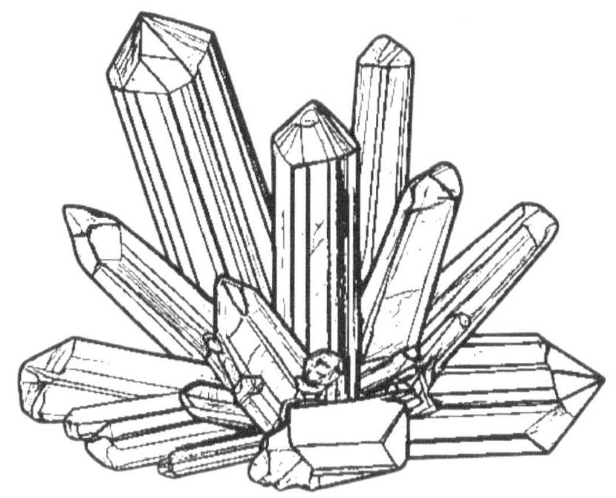

Introduction to Opal

Opal is a mesmerizing gemstone known for its iridescent play of colors, symbolizing creativity, inspiration, and emotional healing. This stone's beauty and mystical aura have long captivated people, making it a cherished stone in jewelry and spiritual practices alike.

Properties and Uses of Opal

Opal is revered for its ability to enhance creativity and stimulate the imagination. It is a stone of inspiration, encouraging self-expression and promoting spontaneity. Opal also facilitates emotional healing, helping to release past trauma and bring about positive transformation.

Cleansing and Charging Opal

To maintain Opal's vibrant energy, cleanse it gently using methods like moonlight, sage smudging, or placing it on a bed of sea salt. Charging Opal can be done under the light of the full moon or by placing it with clear quartz crystals to amplify its energies.

Opal Spells

Creativity Boost Spell

Purpose: To enhance creative inspiration.

Materials: Opal, purple candle, artistic tools.

Instructions: Light the purple candle, hold the Opal, and engage in creative activities while allowing inspiration to flow freely.

Inspiration and Insight Spell

Purpose: To gain inspiration and insight.

Materials: Opal, white candle.

Instructions: Light the white candle, hold the Opal, and meditate while focusing on receiving inspiration and insights.

Communication Enhancement Spell

Purpose: To enhance communication skills.

Materials: Opal, blue candle.

Instructions: Light the blue candle, hold the Opal, and visualize clear and effective communication in your interactions.

Self-Expression Spell

Purpose: To enhance self-expression.

Materials: Opal, yellow candle.

Instructions: Light the yellow candle, hold the Opal, and express yourself creatively through writing, art, or speaking.

Confidence Boost Spell

Purpose: To boost self-confidence.

Materials: Opal, orange candle.

Instructions: Light the orange candle, hold the Opal, and affirm your self-worth and confidence.

Dream Enhancement Spell

Purpose: To enhance dreams and intuition.

Materials: Opal, blue candle.

Instructions: Light the blue candle, hold the Opal, and place it near your bed to enhance dreams and intuition during sleep.

Emotional Healing Spell

Purpose: To heal emotional wounds and promote emotional balance.

Materials: Opal, pink candle, healing crystals.

Instructions: Light the pink candle, hold the Opal, and place healing crystals around you while visualizing emotional wounds healing and emotional balance being restored.

Manifestation of Desires Spell

Purpose: To manifest your desires.

Materials: Opal, green candle, list of desires.

Instructions: Light the green candle, hold the Opal, and focus on your desires while visualizing them manifesting into reality.

Love and Compassion Spell

Purpose: To attract love and foster compassion.

Materials: Opal, pink candle, heart-shaped item.

Instructions: Light the pink candle, hold the Opal, and visualize love and compassion filling your heart and life.

Positive Energy Spell

Purpose: To attract positive energy.

Materials: Opal, yellow candle.

Instructions: Light the yellow candle, hold the Opal, and focus on attracting positive energy into your life.

Protection Spell

Purpose: To protect against negativity.

Materials: Opal, black candle.

Instructions: Light the black candle, hold the Opal, and visualize it forming a protective shield around you.

Emotional Stability Spell

Purpose: To achieve emotional stability.

Materials: Opal, green candle.

Instructions: Light the green candle, hold the Opal, and visualize emotional stability and harmony.

Balance and Harmony Spell

Purpose: To restore balance and harmony.

Materials: Opal, blue candle.

Instructions: Light the blue candle, hold the Opal, and visualize balance and harmony in all aspects of your life.

Creativity Flow Spell

Purpose: To enhance creative flow.

Materials: Opal, purple candle, artistic tools.

Instructions: Light the purple candle, hold the Opal, and engage in creative activities while feeling inspired.

Wisdom and Insight Spell

Purpose: To gain wisdom and insight.

Materials: Opal, indigo candle.

Instructions: Light the indigo candle, hold the Opal, and meditate on gaining wisdom and insight.

Stress Relief Spell

Purpose: To alleviate stress.

Materials: Opal, white candle.

Instructions: Light the white candle, hold the Opal, and visualize stress melting away, leaving you feeling calm and relaxed.

Luck Enhancement Spell

Purpose: To enhance overall luck.

Materials: Opal, green candle, lucky charm.

Instructions: Light the green candle, hold the Opal, and place the lucky charm near it while visualizing luck flowing into your life.

Decision Making Spell

Purpose: To aid in decision-making.

Materials: Opal, blue candle, list of options.

Instructions: Light the blue candle, hold the Opal, and focus on gaining clarity and insight into your decisions.

Self-Discovery Spell

Purpose: To promote self-discovery.

Materials: Opal, purple candle, journal.

Instructions: Light the purple candle, hold the Opal, and journal about your thoughts and insights into self-discovery.

Aura Cleansing Spell

Purpose: To cleanse and purify your aura.

Materials: Opal, white candle, sage.

Instructions: Light the white candle, hold the Opal, and burn sage while visualizing your aura being cleansed and purified.

Physical Healing Spell

Purpose: To aid in physical healing.

Materials: Opal, red candle.

Instructions: Light the red candle, hold the Opal, and visualize healing energy flowing through your body.

Patience and Tolerance Spell

Purpose: To cultivate patience and tolerance.

Materials: Opal, blue candle.

Instructions: Light the blue candle, hold the Opal, and affirm patience and tolerance in your interactions.

Success in Endeavors Spell

Purpose: To attract success in endeavors.

Materials: Opal, gold candle.

Instructions: Light the gold candle, hold the Opal, and visualize success and achievement in your endeavors.

Spiritual Growth Spell

Purpose: To stimulate spiritual growth.

Materials: Opal, purple candle.

Instructions: Light the purple candle, hold the Opal, and meditate on spiritual insights and growth.

Opal is a stone of creativity, inspiration, and emotional healing, celebrated for its iridescent beauty and mystical properties. By incorporating these spells into your practice, you can harness Opal's energy to enhance creativity, promote emotional healing, and attract positivity into your life. Embrace the enchanting power of Opal as you nurture your creativity, gain insights, and foster emotional well-being. Each spell deepens your connection to this captivating gemstone, guiding you on a path of personal transformation and spiritual growth.

Jade

Introduction to Jade

Jade is a revered stone known for its healing and protective properties, as well as its association with prosperity and harmony. This lustrous green gemstone has been cherished for centuries in various cultures for its beauty and mystical properties.

Properties of Jade

Jade is known for its ability to promote harmony and balance. It is a stone of prosperity, attracting abundance and good fortune. Jade also supports emotional healing, bringing tranquility and peace to the wearer.

Cleansing and Charging Jade

To keep Jade working at its best, cleanse it regularly by placing it in saltwater, smudging with sage, or burying it in the earth. Charging Jade can be done under moonlight or with other crystals like Clear Quartz to amplify its energies.

Jade Spells

Harmony Spell

Purpose: To promote harmony in relationships.

Materials: Jade, pink candle, photo of loved ones.

Instructions: Light the pink candle, hold the Jade, and visualize harmony and understanding in your relationships.

Prosperity Spell

Purpose: To attract prosperity and abundance.

Materials: Jade, green candle, prosperity herbs.

Instructions: Light the green candle, hold the Jade, and sprinkle prosperity herbs around it while visualizing a steady flow of prosperity.

Emotional Healing Spell

Purpose: To heal emotional wounds.

Materials: Jade, blue candle, soothing music.

Instructions: Light the blue candle, hold the Jade, and listen to soothing music while visualizing emotional wounds healing.

Luck Enhancement Spell

Purpose: To enhance luck and good fortune.

Materials: Jade, yellow candle.

Instructions: Light the yellow candle, hold the Jade, and visualize opportunities for luck and good fortune coming your way.

Protection Spell

Purpose: To protect against negative energies.

Materials: Jade, black candle.

Instructions: Light the black candle, hold the Jade, and visualize it forming a protective shield around you.

Peace and Tranquility Spell

Purpose: To promote inner peace and tranquility.

Materials: Jade, white candle.

Instructions: Light the white candle, hold the Jade, and focus on feeling calm and peaceful.

Love Attraction Spell

Purpose: To attract love into your life.

Materials: Jade, pink candle, rose quartz.

Instructions: Light the pink candle, hold the Jade, and place the rose quartz near it while visualizing love entering your life.

Courage and Strength Spell

Purpose: To boost courage and inner strength.

Materials: Jade, red candle.

Instructions: Light the red candle, hold the Jade, and affirm your courage and strength.

Wisdom and Insight Spell

Purpose: To gain wisdom and insight.

Materials: Jade, purple candle.

Instructions: Light the purple candle, hold the Jade, and meditate on gaining wisdom and insight.

Health and Vitality Spell

Purpose: To enhance health and vitality.

Materials: Jade, green candle, healing crystal.

Instructions: Light the green candle, hold the Jade, and place the healing crystal near it while visualizing vibrant health.

Prosperity Flow Spell

Purpose: To attract a steady flow of prosperity.

Materials: Jade, gold candle, written prosperity affirmations.

Instructions: Light the gold candle, hold the Jade, and focus on prosperity affirmations coming true.

Confidence Boost Spell

Purpose: To boost self-confidence.

Materials: Jade, orange candle.

Instructions: Light the orange candle, hold the Jade, and affirm your self-worth and confidence.

Friendship Spell

Purpose: To attract loyal friendships.

Materials: Jade, pink candle, friendship token.

Instructions: Light the pink candle, hold the Jade, and place the friendship token near it while visualizing loyal friendships.

Patience and Tolerance Spell

Purpose: To cultivate patience and tolerance.

Materials: Jade, blue candle.

Instructions: Light the blue candle, hold the Jade, and affirm patience and tolerance in your interactions.

Spiritual Growth Spell

Purpose: To stimulate spiritual growth.

Materials: Jade, white candle, meditation space.

Instructions: Light the white candle, hold the Jade, and meditate in your sacred space while focusing on spiritual insights.

Balance and Harmony Spell

Purpose: To restore balance and harmony.

Materials: Jade, pink candle.

Instructions: Light the pink candle, hold the Jade, and visualize balance and harmony in your life.

Manifestation Spell

Purpose: To manifest desires into reality.

Materials: Jade, green candle, written manifestation goals.

Instructions: Light the green candle, hold the Jade, and focus on your desires manifesting into reality.

Energy Cleansing Spell

Purpose: To cleanse and purify energy.

Materials: Jade, white candle, incense.

Instructions: Light the white candle, hold the Jade, and burn incense while visualizing energy being cleansed.

Inspiration Spell

Purpose: To receive creative inspiration.

Materials: Jade, purple candle, artistic tools.

Instructions: Light the purple candle, hold the Jade, and engage in creative activities while feeling inspired.

Success Spell

Purpose: To achieve success in endeavors.

Materials: Jade, gold candle.

Instructions: Light the gold candle, hold the Jade, and visualize success and achievement in your endeavors.

Self-Discovery Spell

Purpose: To promote self-discovery.

Materials: Jade, blue candle, journal.

Instructions: Light the blue candle, hold the Jade, and journal about your thoughts and insights into self-discovery.

Intuition Enhancement Spell

Purpose: To enhance intuition.

Materials: Jade, indigo candle.

Instructions: Light the indigo candle, hold the Jade, and meditate on opening your intuition to receive guidance.

Joy and Happiness Spell

Purpose: To attract joy and happiness.

Materials: Jade, yellow candle.

Instructions: Light the yellow candle, hold the Jade, and focus on feelings of joy and happiness filling your heart.

Protection During Travel Spell

Purpose: To protect during journeys.

Materials: Jade, white candle, travel token.

Instructions: Light the white candle, hold the Jade, and place the travel token near it while visualizing safe travels.

Jade is a stone of harmony, prosperity, and emotional healing, revered for its soothing energy and protective qualities. By incorporating these spells into your practice, you can harness Jade's energy to promote harmony, attract prosperity, and foster emotional well-being. Embrace the calming power of Jade as you cultivate balance, attract positivity, and nurture your spiritual growth. Each spell deepens your connection to this revered gemstone, guiding you on a path of inner peace and fulfillment.

As we conclude our journey through the enchanting world of crystals, we reflect on the profound energies and magic they have brought into our lives.

Each crystal has unique qualities—whether it's the protective strength of Obsidian, the loving embrace of Rose Quartz, or the empowering courage of Tiger's Eye.

These spells have not only shown us how to harness the inherent properties of each crystal but have also deepened our connection to our intentions, dreams, and inner selves. As you continue to explore and work with these crystals, may you find inspiration, healing, and transformation.

Remember, the power of crystals lies not only in their beauty and metaphysical properties but also in the intention and love with which you use them. Let this book serve as a guide and companion on your journey of spiritual growth and manifestation.

May your path be illuminated by the light of crystals, guiding you towards fulfillment, peace, and abundance.